Mohan *and* Muhammad

Mohan *and* Muhammad

Gandhi, Jinnah and the Break-up of British India

MEGHNAD DESAI

RUPA

Published by
Rupa Publications India Pvt. Ltd 2025
161-B/4, Gulmohar House,
Yusuf Sarai Community Centre,
New Delhi 110049

Sales centres:
Bengaluru Chennai
Hyderabad Kolkata Mumbai

P-ISBN: 978-93-7003-213-2
E-ISBN: 978-93-7003-729-8

First impression 2025

10 9 8 7 6 5 4 3 2 1

The moral right of the author has been asserted.

Printed in India

For
Baroness Shreela Flather (1934–2024)
A woman pioneer of India and Pakistan
The first to become a member of the House of Lords from the
Conservative Party in 1990

❧

Note: I, Meghnad Desai, became the first Lord of Indian origin appointed by the Labour Party in 1991.

CONTENTS

AUTHOR'S NOTE

It is difficult, almost 80 years since India became independent, to think of India and Pakistan as well as Bangladesh as one single entity. Yet that was the India I was born in, and was a child witness to Independence, as it came with the tragedy of Partition. Before 1947, Peshawar was the town where our favourite film stars Dilip Kumar and Raj Kapoor came from, and Lahore was where Dev Anand, the heartthrob of millions, graduated from. Now they are in what is thought of as alien territory.

For the generation growing up now, it will come as a surprise that once, Gandhi and Jinnah fought together from the same platform for the freedom of India—the country they were both born in—indeed in the same province of Gujarat.

I have tried to tell here the story of the heroic though tragic outcome of India's struggle for independence in which these two Gujarati young men—both barristers from London—collaborated, negotiated and discussed till the very bitter end when independence came, but with Partition. In one sense, they both failed in what they had spent the best years of their lives struggling for. They ended up creating two nation-states instead of their single motherland.

I tell this story which I cannot forget, and hope that neither will you when you read it.

Meghnad Desai

BEFORE THE BEGINNINGS

Mohandas Karamchand Gandhi, aka Mahatma Gandhi or Gandhiji or Bapu (Father), is one of the most well-known persons not only in India but in the world as well. There are, by one calculation, statues of Gandhi in 250 places. There is a statue of him in Parliament Square in London, in Geneva, in Cardiff and in Manchester. There is one in Washington, D.C. There is his memorial at the Raj Ghat in Delhi, and in many other towns, His face smiles at us from the currency notes in India. Around the world, his birthday 2 October, or the day of his assassination 30 January, are remembered.

The statue of Gandhi in Parliament Square is not the only one of a non-British politician. Gandhi is facing straight ahead across a busy road at the gates to the Old Palace Yard which admit cars of MPs to Parliament. There is a statue of Nelson Mandela on Gandhi's right hand. There is also a statue of Jan Smuts of South Africa—who Gandhi had to negotiate with to secure the rights of Indian immigrants living in Transvaal in South Africa—a little distance away on Gandhi's Left. Thus you can see the history of Apartheid and the struggle against it over a century in that triad of Smuts, Gandhi and Mandela. Across the length of the Square, in front of Gandhi, though with his face turned away towards the distant English Channel horizon, stands Winston Churchill, Gandhi's arch-critic. There is a statue of Lloyd George, who was prime minister during the First World War and the Noncooperation Movement led by Gandhi. That reminds you of the British Empire and Gandhi's long struggle against it. But the climax of that struggle was the Partition of India.

What is missing from Parliament Square is a statue of Jinnah who can claim to be the creator of Pakistan. Not that there has not been a demand for such a statue, but somehow Jinnah is not thought to be worthy of that honour. In many ways, Jinnah is cast as the villain of the dispute that led to the Partition of British India, and the creation of Pakistan.

A similar fate was suffered by Jinnah in the area of film biography. Lord (Richard) Attenborough's film *Gandhi* was a roaring success around the world, and won many awards. The film made on Jinnah in 1998, starring Christopher Lee and directed by Jamil Dehlvi, was released in London, but was banned in both India and Pakistan! It was a good film (as I can attest, having been present at its premiere in Leicester Square), but it failed to be widely watched due to the idea in India that Jinnah was the creator of Pakistan, India's archenemy nation, and it being therefore banned. In Pakistan, it was also banned because he was portrayed as not a sufficiently orthodox Muslim for a Father of the Muslim nation. He was shown drinking alcohol and smoking. He was obviously either too evil, or not shown in his human perfection!

Either way, Jinnah cannot win. Gandhi and Jinnah are polar opposites in what passes for national histories of the neighbours— India and Pakistan. It is taken for granted by Gandhi's biographers that they must have been antagonists from the moment they came into contact. Thus Ramachandra Guha, the author, in his excellent two-volume biography of Gandhi, mentions a letter Jinnah wrote to him while he was in South Africa, i.e. before they had met in person. Guha immediately says in this first mention of Jinnah, 'also a Gujarati lawyer who, in the 1930s and 1940s became Gandhi's most implacable Indian adversary', before speculating on what the letter could have been about.[1] Of course, what Guha says about their relationship in the 1930s and 1940s is true, but there is a lot more before we get to that stage, and indeed, a fascinating story of how they got there.

My idea in writing this book is not to redo the biographies of these two very well 'biographed' men. I wish also to avoid a retrospective treatment, where we already start from a knowledge of how their story ended. In fact, through most of the years of their lives, excepting the final one, there was no Partition of India and no Pakistan. Both had spent most of their adult lives fighting for self-government for India. It is difficult for all but people from a very old cohort within the current populations of India and Pakistan to believe that Jinnah was a doughty fighter for **Indian** independence, as, of course, was Gandhi. It is precisely in how they cooperated and then interlocuted, but with little agreement, that encapsulates the tragedy which accompanied British India's Independence and the Partition. I hope to proceed by exploring their lives forward from their childhood, and not backward from how they ended. To understand their lives as they were lived in tandem is key to understanding India and its history.

It is tricky to speak of India in this period, because pre-1947 India is no longer there. It is also difficult to imagine that the leaders of the Indian National Congress liked British rule, and indeed, their hope, at least until 1929, was not for Independence,

---

[1]Guha, Ramachandra, *Gandhi Before India*, Penguin Random House, Gurgaon, 2013, pp. 129.

but for more representative opportunities under British rule. When Mohandas Gandhi raised an Indian force of ambulance workers during the Boer War (1897–1901) in South Africa, his argument was based on the duties of Indians to repay the debt they owed to the Empire. Thus Guha quotes Gandhi saying, 'I held then (in 1890s) that India could achieve complete emancipation only within and through the British Empire.'[2] As he left South Africa for the last time in 1914, Gandhi expressed his hope that the Europeans (i.e. the Boers and the British) of South Africa (would) take a humanitarian and Imperial view of the Indian question. Here, the word 'Imperial' is for the British Empire whom Gandhi trusted to be more just towards the Indians than were the Boers, who were Dutch by origin and more 'racist' compared to the British settlers in South Africa.

The name may have stayed, but India before Independence was not the same as India after Independence. There are not many people left alive who remember that there was once an India which included what is now Pakistan and Bangladesh (and until 1935, even Burma, now Myanmar, was included in India). Thus, few today would know that Lahore has a historical importance for Old India—that is, both India and Pakistan—in several ways; Nehru, as Congress president, took oath on 26 December 1929 on the banks of the river Ravi in Lahore that the Indian National Congress would fight for the goal of full freedom (*Purna Swaraj*), unless it was granted by the British within one month—if not, henceforth to celebrate 26 January as Independence Day. (Later in 1950, it was the day India became

---

[2]Guha, Ramachandra, *Gandhi Before India*, Penguin Random House, Gurgaon, 2013, p. 138.

a Sovereign Democratic Republic, but this was new India, not Old India.) Ten years later, in March 1940 in Lahore, the All India Muslim League passed a resolution to denote the group of Muslim-majority provinces in the northwest plus Bengal and Assam as a separate Muslim entity (popularly called 'Pakistan' at the time, but not in the Resolution itself). Lahore was also the capital of the Great Sikh Empire of Ranjit Singh, the last independent Non-Muslim, Non-Hindu kingdom in an India that was even older than the British India we shall discuss. This variety of circumstances to which the word 'India' refers makes it tricky to speak of it over the last hundred years or longer. So I shall use 'All India' or 'British India' for pre-Partition India in this book, wherever necessary, to avoid any misunderstanding. Of course, even in those days, there was an Indian India where kings and princes ruled under British paramountcy. As to pre-1857 India, we shall not have occasion to refer to it.

My effort in this book will be to show the commonalities, rather than just the contrasts, between the lives and careers of Gandhi and Jinnah; the many ways in which their lives trod common, if not identical, paths, and how they were together in British Indian politics for nearly a quarter of a century. And then, how they parted ways but only to become the two key interlocutors at the final moment, the two representatives of the ideas of India and Pakistan. While the final decision had to be made by the viceroy (Lord Mountbatten) in 1947, the parleys between Gandhi and Jinnah earlier in the decade were closely followed as preparing the way for it. In a vital sense which still makes their story relevant, they both failed to achieve their objective. Their failure has shaped the more recent history of South Asia, i.e. Old India.

There is also another angle which, by now, after all these years, can be pursued. This is to probe, now and then, what the Indian struggle for independence looked like from the British point of view. It is easily assumed that the independence struggle faced a monolith in the form of the British Raj. But there were differences— as between the London end with the India Office, and Delhi (or earlier, Calcutta) where the government of India sat. At home in London, there was a Parliament with rival parties; not all agreed on the same view of Indian affairs. Even within parties, there were rivalries—the dislike between Balfour and Curzon, which made the latter resign; and it had nothing to do with Curzon's decision to partition Bengal, but more the dispute between Curzon and his commander-in-chief of the Indian Army Lord Kitchener.[3]

British India was important enough for the British to appoint only scions of the aristocracy—lords or earls or viscounts—as viceroys. Lord Irwin was raised to this title from being Edward Wood when he was chosen to be viceroy to India, thus getting an 'accelerated title' while waiting to succeed his father Lord Halifax when the latter would die. It would not do to have a common or garden-variety gentleman to rule India. So wherever relevant, I refer to developments at the London end to put the Indian struggle in perspective.

The lives of Gandhi and Jinnah have been much written about. Biographies of Gandhi still appear despite the availability of scores of attempts already. His *Collected Writings* take up a hundred volumes, and there may yet be more to come. There are a few biographies of Jinnah, but not that many. Facts about

---

[3]Mosley, Leonard, *Curzon: The End of an Epoch*, Readers Union, Longman Green & co., London, 1961.

Jinnah's childhood are not definite, as even his date of birth is disputed. He was, by nature, not given to confessional writings or instructing his readers in all facets of life as Gandhi was. Nor was he given to writing letters to the famous as Gandhi did to Tolstoy and Hitler, for example. So we have to do with a skeletal knowledge of Jinnah, and use some imagination to fathom his thoughts. He was certainly not the Jinnah as he has now come to be portrayed. The only book so far that I know on Gandhi and Jinnah is by M.J. Akbar. It is excellent as one would expect, but it confines itself principally to the Partition period as well as Gandhi's religion.[4] I have referred a lot to a biography of Jinnah written in 1945 by Sayyid. The advantage of having access to this book is that being a pre-Partition publication, it is not retrospective. Jinnah and Gandhi were not cast in their present images.

Unlikely Twins

Biographies of the famous are always written in a retrospective mode. Thus it is often claimed that the greatness later achieved was implicit in the young man or woman. (A popular Hindi song written soon after Gandhi's death begins with the line [as translated]: 'In Porbandar Gujarat was born a Rishi (a holy Indian mendicant) whom his parents gave the name Mohandas Karamchand Gandhi.' To call a newborn baby a Rishi is to give the end away, as if it was inevitable, to say the least.) It is then difficult to see the person as moving forward, not knowing where he will

---

[4]Akbar, M.J., *Gandhi's Hinduism: The Struggle Against Jinnah's Islam*, Bloomsbury, London, 2020.

end up. To see the lives of Gandhi and Jinnah in a prospective way, beginning from childhood, I will refer to them, to begin with, by their first names, Mohan for Gandhi and Muhammad for Jinnah. This is not to disrespect them, but to remind ourselves that once in their lives, they were unknown, and did not foresee their future. As they get older, I shall refer to them by their names—Mohandas or Muhammad Ali, or their initials (MKG for Gandhi, and MAJ for Jinnah).

Another difficulty with writing about the two is that Gandhi's reputation as a Mahatma and 'Father of the Nation' in India makes even the slightest criticism of his thoughts, behaviour and decisions immediately disputed. His perfection is taken for granted. But in writing a history, one has to be constantly aware that these men faced human challenges which they dealt with in their personal, human ways. They were neither perfect nor omniscient. Of course, they achieved greatness, but that is our ex-post judgement.

Whatever the choice of perspective, in one part of global history, Gandhi and Jinnah are twinned together, but as irreconcilable opposites. But what is not so widely known, though it is no secret, is that their lives were not only lived in parallel, but that there are many similarities between the two. They were both from Gujarati-speaking families. Their families originated from the Kathiawar region of Gujarat in western India. Gandhi was born on 2 October 1869 in Porbandar, a port on the Arabian Sea. His father Karamchand was the diwan (chief minister) to the prince (thakore) of Porbandar. When Mohandas, his last child, was five, his father moved to Rajkot—another larger town in Kathiawar. He became chief justice of the court.[5]

---

[5]Hunt, James D., *Gandhi in London*, Promilla Books, New Delhi, 2012.

Rajkot was also the town where Muhammad's grandfather Poonjabhai came from. It has to be noted that the name 'Poonjabhai' is an unusual name for a Gujarati. 'Poonja' means rubbish—what you sweep away. His father was called Zeenabhai. 'Zeena' means fine, as in a fine stitch for an embroidery. It looks like a description of a small man, but more likely it is because in Gujarati families (and no doubt across Old India), newborn sons were often given a dismissive name to avoid the Evil Eye. It was a safeguard against the danger of infant mortality in those simpler days. Mohan was called Munia by his sister Raliat.

These names would be dropped when the child grew to an older age. But in Jinnah's case, the dismissive names seem to have stayed. It could have reflected their *jati* status. The family traded in goods including fish and other seafood, which is thought to be an occupation that is looked down upon by caste Hindus. (Other accounts say that it was a general export business selling hides and skins, and so on.) If true, this would tell us that as Gujarati names go, the Jinnahs were 'gandhis', i.e. grocers, more truly than the Gandhis themselves, who were diwans! So while they were of the Halai Lohana jati from Pilani near Rajkot, i.e. the Bania caste, the same as Gandhi, they were probably treated more as what are now called, in Modern India, the Other Backward Castes. But they were prospering in their business. Poonjabhai moved to Karachi where he built a large business. (Later, the family seems to have moved to Bombay, but may have gone back to Karachi. Muhammad did go to a school in Bombay for some years in his academic career. Details are lacking.)

It is possible that in order to raise their social status (Sanskritize, as the equivalent move among Hindus has been named by the distinguished sociologist M.N. Srinivas), the family converted from Hinduism to adopt the Ismaili sect of Islam. There is a small but prosperous community of Khojas, as these Ismaili Muslims are called, in Gujarat. The Aga Khan is the spiritual leader of the Ismailis. It is my conjecture, of course, but it may well have been that having prospered in the business, the family decided to improve their social status by conversion to the Ismaili sect. The Ismailis have been said to be like half-Hindu and half-Muslim, and culturally like the Parsees.[6] Later in life, Muhammad Ali Jinnah was described as a Shia Muslim, though he was never very religious (which may surprise Indians as well as Pakistanis).

In any case, Muhammad, with a proper dignified name Muhammad Ali Jinnah (the father's diminutive name being transformed into a dignified last name), was born in Karachi—his parents' first son after three daughters—on Christmas Day in 1876, making him just seven years younger than Mohan. (One source mentions his birthday as being on 20 October 1875.)[7] He was one of seven children, but some sources also say that he was the oldest of seven children. His best-known sibling was a younger sister Fatema, who became his lifelong carer. This makes both Gandhi and Jinnah Victorians as the Queen Empress was then the ruler of India. They both went to London to become barristers, Mohan to the Inner Temple and Muhammad to the nearby Lincoln's Inn—Mohan just short of his 19th birthday, and Muhammad when he was just sixteen. Mohan hurried home in 1891 as Muhammad arrived in London.

---

[6]Goradia, Prafull, *Jinnah Helped the Hindus and Other Explorations*, Vitasta, New Delhi, 2020.

[7]Wolpert, Stanley, *Jinnah of Pakistan*, Oxford University Press, New York, 1984, p. 5.

In both their cases, it was a family friend or adviser who suggested that the young man be sent to London to become a barrister as that did not require a college degree. In case of Mohan, it was Mavji Dave, a family friend, who made the suggestion. In Muhammad's case, his father had a British friend Sir Frederick Leigh Croft, himself a barrister, who made the suggestion. (Another story is that Sir Frederick was the general manager of a managing agency Douglas Graham and Company, which did business with Poonjabhai, and Muhammad was sent to London to work with the London head office as an apprentice. Then he is supposed to have got bored and moved to law.)[8]

There is some misunderstanding as to what these Inns of Court were. Recently (in March 2023), a high official, the lieutenant governor of Jammu and Kashmir, said (by way of encouraging the young students he was addressing) that Mahatma Gandhi had no college degree and still achieved great things. As he was from the current ruling party BJP which was opposed by the Congress, Tushar Gandhi, a grandson of the Mahatma, retorted that this was not the case as he had been to a college—the Inner Temple. This is to impute modern features to an ancient institution. The Inns of Court were dining clubs, not colleges. Jinnah has been quoted as saying that he chose Lincoln's Inn because a likeness of Prophet Muhammad is inscribed as one of the great law-givers on the front facade of the inn. (Given the recent Islamist fervour, such an image would be objected to by devout Muslims, but no one seems to have done so with Lincoln's Inn.) This is indeed so (I saw it frequently as Lincoln's Inn is near the LSE where I worked), but still, Lincoln's Inn was where he had his required

---

[8]Ibid., p. 7.

number of dinners with alcoholic drinks and all. We are not told whether Muhammad partook of the drinks.

Mohan tells us in his autobiography (*The Story of My Experiments with Truth*, hereafter *SMET*) how these inns operated:

> There were two conditions which had to be fulfilled before a student was formally called to the bar: 'keeping terms' twelve terms equivalent to about three years, and passing examinations. 'Keeping terms' meant eating one's terms, i.e. attending at least six out of about twenty-four dinners in a term. But as someone who did not partake of alcohol, he was a popular fourth person to have at a dinner table. As he says, 'Two bottles of wine were allowed to each group of four, and as I did not touch them, I was ever in demand to form a quarter so that three might empty two bottles.'[9]

The inns did not teach their members, but were places where potential barristers socialized with seniors of their profession. A certain number of dinners were required to maintain membership. Examinations were regulated by the number of terms you had kept with the most difficult subjects in the third set of examinations, and candidates who passed them, having also had the dinners, were 'called to the Bar', qualified to practise as barristers. Muhammad was the youngest person (at that date) from India to be called to the Bar.[10]

Both Mohan and Muhammad were, later in life, proud to describe themselves as English barristers. In case of both, one can

[9]Gandhi, M.K., *An Autobiography: or The Story of My Experiments with Truth*, Mahadev Desai (trans.), Navjivan, Ahmedabad, 1927/2004, p. 73.
[10]Hunt, James D., *Gandhi in London*, Promilla Books, New Delhi, 2012.

see, as I hope to show, that they grew up into adulthood during their stay in London, and indeed, thought of London fondly all their lives. Jinnah even returned to London when he got fed up with British Indian politics in the late 1920s. Gandhi had lots of opportunities to visit London while he worked in South Africa between 1893 and 1914, and said later that if he were not engaged in Indian politics, he would have preferred to live in London.

Their lives diverge during their twenties—with Mohan going off to South Africa, while Muhammad thrived in Bombay as a pleader. Their experience on returning from London to India (to Bombay, as it was then called), in both cases, was similar. Each found it hard to find any clients who would engage them. Mohan found that he was nervous when the chance came for him to plead in court. Muhammad had no such fear, but it took him two years before a break came in his professional career. Mohan found, through family contacts, that he could go to South Africa where someone could use his services. Off he went, and one way or another, things occurred in his life, and he spent altogether 21 years in South Africa. Muhammad stayed, prospered as a barrister, and plunged into Indian politics—making his mark early in the Indian National Congress (hereafter Congress).

The world was changing, though ever so slowly, from our perspective. The real change in Britain (as in some other Western countries) was the growth of franchise. In the UK, the franchise covered only two per cent of the adult male population in late eighteenth century when the French Revolution erupted. You had to be paying a rate (a tax) to qualify to vote. From then on, through the nineteenth century, the franchise was extended to lower income groups such as urban property-holders. By the

1880s, the better-off men from the working classes had a right to vote. The Liberal Party (Whigs, as they were popularly known) were taking the lead in spreading the franchise.

There had been a limited amount of reform in India, introducing a modicum of urban government in the late nineteenth century. Of course, the Indian National Congress had been inaugurated in 1885, but it was very much a gathering of loyal subjects of the Empire—the more prosperous and professional ones—who attended the annual meetings of the Congress. Dadabhai Naoroji was able to benefit from the spread of the franchise in Britain by contesting for the Parliament on a Liberal Party ticket. He had a vote, and could run for Parliament (there was no racial barrier).

In India, there was a council to advise the viceroy in Delhi. This was an appointed (not an elected) council, but change was imminent. Lord Curzon had expanded the membership of the Viceroy's Council by adding what we would consider civil society representatives—appointed, not elected. That was during the Conservative government of the marquess of Salisbury, in the last decade of the nineteenth century.

The Liberals won a decisive victory in 1905, which ushered in a change in India as well. They were sympathetic to Indian demands for some representation. Lord John Morley was secretary of state for India, and he introduced voting for the Imperial Legislative Council. There was a property qualification, of course, but he also introduced separate electorates for Hindus and Muslims. This move has been much criticized by historians as sowing the seeds of communal division. Yet the British perceived even their own society in terms of groups defined by religion, or even sects within Christianity. Thus, eligibility for jobs in the universities of Oxford or Cambridge depended on being Anglican, and swearing allegiance to the Articles of the Church of England, which disqualified Catholics and Methodists.

The British initiated a census in India in 1871, and began tabulating population numbers by religion as well as gender. They designated the population as Hindus and Muslims, Parsees and Christians, and so on. So they introduced separate electorates for Muslims and Hindus to elect representatives to the Viceroy's Council. Given that the incomes were, on the average, higher among Hindus (a larger middle class, more Western education), the income qualification was lower for Muslims than it was for Hindus.

It was in this context that Muhammad Ali Jinnah entered Indian politics. Mohandas Gandhi was fighting for the rights of Indians in South Africa with a less sympathetic ruling order.

Each earned a reputation as a politician fighting for the cause of Indians. Again, it will sound strange to young readers (i.e. anyone under 60) to refer to Jinnah as being in **Indian** politics. But Jinnah was, after all, the Son of India—though he also became the Father of Pakistan. Both Gandhi in South Africa and Jinnah in India were part of the Congress. They met up in 1915 when Mohan returned to India, and for almost 10 years, they worked together, often appearing on the same platforms. This was the time where Muhammad was regularly active in the Congress. Mohan was seen at Congress gatherings as and when he was in India while he was active in South Africa. He joined Congress activities in India upon his return in 1915. Jinnah got elected to the Viceroy's Council.

In 1919, impressed by India's contribution to the British victory in the First World War, Edwin Montagu, secretary of state for

India, announced British plans to begin the process whereby there would be a movement, slow and steady, towards self-government in India. There were to be directly elected representatives in provincial assemblies with power to run the ministries in some 'minor' areas. This opened up a scope for Hindus and Muslims in their separate electorates to bid for representation. Jinnah became involved in this development.

During the 1920s, their ways parted. Mohan became the undisputed leader of the Congress, which he converted into a mass political party, rather than a polite Constitutionalist lobbying society which it had hitherto been, and committed it to the Khilafat movement which was begun by two young Muslim leaders—the brothers Mohammad Ali (the same who recruited Jinnah into the Muslim League) and Shaukat Ali, both England-returned. Mohammad was put off by Mohan introducing a Hindu religion in politics as he was a Liberal Constitutionalist, and had never shown any interest in religion. Muhammad was unwilling to address Mohan as 'Mahatma', and quit the Congress. From 1920 onwards, Mohan stayed the leader of the Congress, even when he ceased to be a member of the party in the 1930s. His was the final word on all Congress matters almost till the advent of Independence. Jinnah continued his project of securing adequate representation for Muslims in any scheme of a Constitution for a future self-governing India.

But in the meantime, Great Britain, after some years of short-lived Cabinets, got its act together, and the Conservative Party came to power in 1924. It stayed in power one way or another (except a short rule of two years by the Labour Party) until 1945. They ignored Gandhi's tactics of direct action, and pushed along constitutional lines. This changed the context in which the representatives would be elected. Instead of separate electorates, there could be a joint electorate. MAJ abandoned his Lucknow formula and the separate electorates. He proposed joint electorates. Yet Congress did not concede. Congress was, at that time, influenced by the Hindu Mahasabha, a Hindu nationalist and anti-Muslim political party. MAJ was frustrated and returned to London. He resumed his career as a barrister, and was in demand to plead before the Privy Council (which was the highest Court of Appeal in the British Empire at that time).

Meanwhile, the unstoppable juggernaut of British Constitution-mongering went on relentlessly. A commission with members of both the Houses of Parliament was constituted—headed by Lord Simon—to review the work of the Montagu-Chelmsford Reforms of 1919. Such a review by both Houses was legislated for in the original act. Congress decided to boycott the Simon Commission on the grounds that it did not include an Indian member (which would not have been possible without a new act of Parliament), but the commission finished its work and submitted a voluminous report.[11] Then, there was an acceleration in British activity, and a Round Table Conference was held in London with its inaugural session in November 1930, where all the various groups which constituted Indian society—political parties, Hindus, Muslims, trade unions, women, native princes, untouchables—were invited to discuss India's future. Muhammad Ali Jinnah was invited in his individual capacity as a former member of the Imperial Legislative Council, and a Muslim leader.

---

[11]Desai, Meghnad, *The Rediscovery of India*, Penguin Random House, Gurgaon, India, 2009.

He attended the opening session and the second session. Congress refused to attend the first session on the grounds that it should be the sole invitee, representing all of India. After a delay, Congress agreed to participate, having realized that it was missing out on taking part in an important constitutional discussion, and sent MKG as its sole delegate for the second round in 1931. This was the only time Gandhi travelled outside India since he returned from South Africa. The conference had one more round, where neither MKG nor MAJ was present.[12]

The next step was when the British Parliament enacted the Government of India Act, 1935, based on the discussions at the Round Table Conference and the work of some British parliamentary delegations, which visited British India. India was to have self-governing provinces under British governors, but at the centre there was to be no self-government yet. Elections were to be held for the provincial legislatures. Jinnah was requested to return to India. He agreed, and led Muslims for the forthcoming elections in British India, scheduled for 1937. The Muslim League won a much smaller proportion of the Muslim seats than it should have done to justify its claim as the sole representative of Muslims. Congress emerged as the largest party in many provinces, and turned down any idea of a coalition with the Muslim League in forming Cabinets. Jinnah realized that Muslims would have to get organized, and concentrated on the twin tasks of building the Muslim League as a parliamentary party and launching a struggle to realize the idea of Pakistan. He was now the undisputed leader of the Muslims. He left London and returned to his Malabar Hill house in Bombay.

---

[12]Hunt, James D., *Gandhi in London*, Promilla Books, New Delhi, 2012.

The last decade of both men's lives was spent on opposite sides of the debate about the shape of British India after the anticipated departure of the British. They both died in 1948 after Independence and the Partition—Mohandas in January and Muhammad in September.

Thus it can be seen that whatever the perspective now, in those 30-odd years before Independence, their lives were intertwined, at first in tandem, and then in opposition to each other. Few are aware today that Muhammad Ali Jinnah was active in Congress before he joined the Muslim League. Mohandas Gandhi entered Congress politics in India later than Muhammad Ali Jinnah. At the midpoint of the first half of the twentieth century, they became representatives of two different viewpoints. The course of the Indian independence movement bifurcated into two streams. But even so, it was touch-and-go till the last few months before August 1947—whether there would be one or two independent nation-states within British India. Only in May 1947 was the Partition decided upon. Jinnah got his 'moth eaten' Pakistan. Gandhi was blamed for being partisan to Pakistan soon after the Partition, and shot by a Hindu nationalist. Jinnah died within just 13 months of the founding of Pakistan. Mohandas Gandhi is hailed as the 'Father of the Nation' in India. Muhammad Ali Jinnah, by a parallel process, deserves to be called the Father of Pakistan. Should his statue also not be in Parliament Square?

Most people will say no.

This may be, it can be argued, because Gandhi, the Mahatma, is a globally iconic figure which Jinnah is not. Even so, not all the people whose statues adorn the Parliament Square are well known, let alone global icons. Jinnah has the rare distinction of having been the first head (as governor-general, equivalent to a head of state) of a new nation. Pakistan was created, *ab initio*, having no history as such before 1947. Like it or not, it was Jinnah's achievement to have negotiated the Partition of British India between 1940, when he formally proposed it, and 1947, when it came into being. Yes, it was at an enormous cost in terms of human lives. This should not be read as solely his fault. The result and the long process preceding the result, if carefully followed, will show that the responsibility has to be shared on all sides.[13]

If you cross the border between India and Pakistan over land at the Wagah Border as I have done, you see on the Indian side a photograph of Gandhi and on the Pakistan side, one of Jinnah. Each is considered the 'Father of the Nation'. One is a Mahatma and the other is Quaid-e-Azam. There was a nation before 1947, which was also called India, but under British Rule—hence British India. After Independence in 1947, it became India and Pakistan. In July 1947, the Independence of India Act was passed by the British Parliament, which gave the name 'India' to the larger area which had a Hindu majority. Pakistan was not named in the title of the act, but its name and territorial extent were detailed in the second article of the act.

The life stories of Mohan and Muhammad revolve around their attempt to secure independence for British India, and end with two nation-states, India and Pakistan, instead of one. How and why this happened is their story which I tell here.

---

[13] I have discussed the Partition in over three chapters in my title: Desai, Meghnad, *The Rediscovery of India*, Penguin Random House, Gurgaon, India, 2009.

ONE

FIRST STEPS TO FOOTSTEPS

If you look at their childhoods—as described by himself in Mohan's case, and reported by others in Muhammad's case—there is little indication as to their subsequent ascent to greatness. They both passed their matriculation at 16, but without registering any outstanding results. Mohan got bored in college, and quit after a year. It is not at all certain what he would have done had his family not decided upon sending him abroad. After Karamchand, Mohan's father, died at the age of 63, the family realized that he had not left a large fortune behind. (Apparently, Karamchand was self-denying. Rumour is that although the thakore [prince] of Porbandar was ready to offer him some land as a gift, Karamchand would not accept more than 400 yards.) Now the family needed someone who could restore their fortunes. Mohan was the only one of Karamchand's three sons who matriculated. Hence the idea was that he should be sent to England to become a barrister. Then, upon returning, he could restore the family fortunes. The Gandhis had been diwans of one kingdom or another in Kathiawar for some generations. As a barrister from London, he was more likely to succeed to the position his father and ancestors had held—as the diwan with some local king—than either of his two older brothers. No such crisis of fortune is mentioned in Muhammad's case. It seems that the family had the means to send their son to London.

What becomes clear at this stage is that the family seemed to play a much larger role in Mohan's life than in Muhammad's. This may be because of Gandhi writing his autobiography in the 1920s, midway through his career, the way he did. I shall come to this later. As for Muhammad, the details of his childhood are scarce. Both had a child-marriage, but while Mohan got formally married at 13, and began a conjugal life with his wife Kastur, Muhammad did not do the same, and the girl he was betrothed to at the age of 15—Amai Bai—died early in his life, while he was abroad. His father died while he was in London, just as Mohan's mother did. Muhammad's mother is not mentioned in his biographies. Muhammad himself never spoke about his family or his childhood, except for his younger sister Fatema. He was a very private person.

Becoming an Adult in England

The leap forward in the lives of both came in England. We know much more about Mohan than about Muhammad in this matter as well. Being a strict vegetarian, Mohan stumbled upon a vegetarian restaurant in Farringdon, not far from the Inner Temple. This introduced him to a group of unusual, unorthodox, radical men and women, vegetarians all, who welcomed him, integrated him into their vegetarian society. Here onwards, Mohan met health faddists, esoteric Christians, people curious to be taught the secrets of Hinduism by him. He met Theosophists—Madam Blavatsky and Annie Besant.

In a way, unlike many other students from India going to Britain who tended to stick with other Indians for company, Mohan met tolerant, non-racist (as we would say nowadays) English people, who were unusual and interesting. They all seemed to have been from the middle class or above. From our present awareness of racism, it is remarkable that not only did Mohan experience no racism, but he also cultivated many White English friends, was able to secure accommodation in good parts of London, and was imbued with a positive, friendly feeling towards English people forever more.

The reason for this is not hard to find. Racism operates in many societies through a filter of class, not just colour. (After all, within India, untouchability is a similar form of rejection of a particular group of people.) A modern British historian Sir David Canadine has written that in Britain, the wealthy, be they Indian or African, suffered no prejudice in their dealings with the locals.[1] Mohan, after all, came from a middle-class family which was prosperous enough to send him to London for further studies. His vegetarianism brought him in touch with political and social radicals, who faced the disapproval of their fellow non-vegetarian Whites. But they were themselves confident in their choices. Mohan was able to find genuine local support for his vegetarianism, and even a scientific argument for it.

Mohan got to know such people, which was rarely experienced by any other Indian visitor of his age; neither Patel nor Nehru, who became his followers in the independence movement and who became barristers in London, reports having done so. He acquired the confidence of writing to Sir Edward Arnold, author of the very popular translation of the Bhagavad Gita in English, titled 'The Song Celestial', about the two of them starting a

---

[1]Canadine, David, *Class in Britain*, Penguin, Middlesex, London, 1998.

Vegetarian Society in West London where they lived. As he wrote in *SMET*,

> Full of the neophyte's zeal for vegetarianism, I decided to start a vegetarian club in my locality of Bayswater. I invited Sir Edward Arnold who lived there, to be Vice-President. Dr Oldfield who was editor of *The Vegetarian* became President. I myself became the Secretary. The club went well for a while. It came to an end in the course of a few months. For I left the locality according to my custom of moving from place to place periodically. But this brief and modest experience gave me some little training in organising and conducting institutions.[2]

This is a boy who could not speak English when he was about to come to England. He came to know and like the English, and they took to him. He found the courage to write, on his own, to a knight and a famous man of his times, to become vice president of a club he was starting. What remarkable confidence! No wonder that in his later life he could easily speak with British ministers and viceroys as an equal.

We also observe that over a long lifetime, his close friends (and they were few, unlike his many followers and fellow Congressmen) were English-speaking White men and women, Christians or Jews. Except for Pranjivan Mehta, who was a relation and who met him upon his arrival in London, he rarely mentioned an Indian as a friend.

Muhammad had a rather normal Indian student experience. He finished his Bar examinations in two, rather than three,

---

[2]Gandhi, M.K., *An Autobiography: or The Story of My Experiments with Truth*, Mahadev Desai (trans.), Navjivan, Ahmedabad, 1927/2004, pp. 54–55.

years—the fastest any Indian student had done it so far. He even had to wait around till he spent enough terms (i.e. had enough dinners) to be called to the Bar. Unlike Mohan, he did not dash back home as soon as he was called to the Bar. He lingered, and enjoyed London. He dabbled in theatre, and played Romeo in a theatre production, according to some sources. He learnt to dress himself in an impeccable English style, and stuck with it most of his life. He went to the gallery of the House of Commons to watch the debates. He was impressed by the Liberal Party, and adopted a monocle, copying Joseph Chamberlain, his political hero back then. He got to know Dadabhai Naoroji, who had won the election to the House of Commons. It has been mentioned that he might have been present in the House of Commons public gallery during Dadabhai's maiden speech. Indian politics was going to be his playground when he got back. He became, in British terms, a Liberal Constitutionalist.

In a rare moment of reminiscing, he told Dr Ashraf of the Aligarh Muslim University in 1921 that 'during the last two years in London, his time was "utilised for further independent studies, for the political career he already had in mind". He also said, 'Fortune smiled on me and I happened to meet several important English liberals with whom I came to understand the doctrine of liberalism. The liberalism of Lord Morley was then in full sway. I grasped that liberalism which became part of my life and thrilled me very much.'[3]

It has been reported that (unusually for him) he also was found pushing a hand cart down the road on Boat Race Night (the traditional annual boat race between Oxford and Cambridge

[3]Bolitho, Hector, *Jinnah: Creator of Pakistan*, John Murray, London, 1954, p. 9.

University students which is often followed by robust enjoyment on the part of the young student spectators), but was let off with just a caution. He returned to India in the autumn of 1896. After a short visit to Karachi, he settled down in Bombay to search for clients who needed his services. It took him a couple of years before he found any.

Responsible Twenties

Mohandas Gandhi: 1891–1915

It is difficult, if not impossible, to think of Mohandas Gandhi as a young man in his twenties. But that was what he was when he got to South Africa. He had not as yet done a proper job, nor earned any income worth speaking of. In 1893, he was just 24 years old, and left his wife and children behind, a second time within five years.

Mohan encountered a different India in South Africa—Muslim merchants from Gujarat and poor indentured labourers from Bihar and Tamil Nadu. Unlike what he saw in England, there was rampant racism between the Whites and the Indians, to say nothing of the native Black Africans. English barrister or no, he was treated like a 'coolie' as he was brown-skinned. He also had to show that he was worth his hire. This took him to Pretoria, out of British-ruled Natal to Boer (Dutch) country in the Transvaal, when he learnt the hard way about White racism towards the non-White—be he an English barrister or not. But he complained and resisted legally and firmly. He refused to suffer silently as other Indians had learnt to do.

A Brief History of South Africa

It is necessary, at this juncture, to relate the history of South Africa as it was in the late nineteenth century.[4]

The Dutch East India Company founded a shipping station at the Cape of Good Hope in 1652. The settlers were mainly Dutch Calvinists who brought a tradition of dissent and resentment against Europe. They called themselves 'Afrikaners' or 'Afrikanders' (people of Africa), and spoke a variant of Dutch which was called Afrikaans. The poorest and most independent among them were called 'trekboers' (alias Boers). They were wandering farmers who went deep into the African territory looking for grazing lands.

During the Anglo-French Wars (1793–1815), the British took possession of the colony. The Cape became a useful naval base on the route to India, which the British were getting into by then. But the latter did not wish to settle there as colonists, unlike the Boers. When the British abolished slavery in 1834, the Boers (who had Black African slaves) began a long march—the *Great Trek*—5,000 Boers with as many slaves across the rivers Orange and Vaal, northeast of the Cape Colony. As Thomas Pakenham, in his history of the Boer War, says 'The *Voortrekkers* (pioneers) quarrelled among themselves, but shared one article of faith: to deny political rights to Africans and Coloured people of mixed race.'[5]

A side effect of the British abolition of slave trade in 1834 was that labourers were recruited on the basis of *indenture*—a

---

[4]I am relying here on the excellent account by Thomas Pakenham in his 1979 book *The Boer War: Historical Note.*

[5]Pakenham, Thomas, *The Boer War*, Weidenfeld and Nicholson, London, 1979, p. xxii.

limited period of tied employment by agreement for a duration of 15 years after which they would be free. India proved to be a major source of such labour (as well as some Chinese from Southeast Asia). The Indian expression for such labour was 'girmitiya'—a corruption of the English word 'agreement'. These labourers came from Bihar, Uttar Pradesh and Tamil Nadu. Some went to the Caribbean islands to replace African slaves, whose supply could not be replenished. Merchants from Gujarat followed these indentured labourers to serve their needs. It was easier for Muslims to travel overseas than it was for caste Hindus.

The British did not extend their rule to the regions where the Boers had gone beyond the Vaal River—the Transvaal; nor did they venture beyond the Orange River where the Orange Free State was set up by the Boers. The rules of governance were kept vague for much of the next 60 years.

But in 1843, the British established a colony in Natal on the eastern end of South Africa. The Voortrekkers did not object. Then in the early 1850s, the independence of the Transvaal and the Orange Free State was recognized by the British. In 1877, the British changed their minds, and annexed the Transvaal with an intention of creating a federation in South Africa. But the locals revolted, and in 1881, Paul Kruger led a rebellion of the Boers and defeated the British in the Battle of Majuba. The Transvaal became independent, but with British oversight of its foreign policy.

So in South Africa during the 1890s, when MKG was there, there were two White European 'nations'—British and Boer (Dutch)—which were not on congenial terms with each other, but also antagonistic, though in a different way, to Asian immigrants and local Africans. The Boers, once in control of two provinces, the Transvaal and the Orange Free State, did not want the British, whom they called 'Uitlander' (foreigners), *to have the right to vote for their Raad* (as their Parliament was called). The Boers, being Calvinists, were Christian fundamentalists, and thought of British Protestants as soft and undeserving. This, after some long twists and turns (which Pakenham covers brilliantly in his book), led to the Boer War between the British and the Boers. Gandhi was to learn the hard way that the differences between the racisms practised by the two European nations were a problem he had to negotiate.

Gandhi in Natal

We can now return to our account of Mohandas Gandhi in his first paid job in Durban, Natal.

It turned out that knowing Gujarati helped him settle the claim he was brought over to solve. By then, he had convinced his hosts, by his conduct in the court of law as well as his general reaction to the experience of racism, that he was tougher than other Indian migrants. He could and did complain formally, rather than silently swallow the insults as the others did. He was about to return to India when it became known that there was new legislation in Natal to deprive Indians of their right to vote and elect the members of the Natal Legislative Assembly. When he asked his host Abdullah Sheth about it, the reply was: 'What can we understand in these matters?' Young as he was compared to his clients, they conceded his primacy in formally approaching the powers that be. He was the only London-trained Indian barrister in Natal, who also could understand the languages the Indians were speaking. He was to remain unique for many more years.

So when, on the eve of his departure, they found they were facing a new attack on their status, they asked him to lead the way. At the very outset, he was not only requested to lead, but those who needed him—the merchants—also acknowledged his obvious superiority in the formal, legal processes of protest. As he wrote, one of the people at his farewell party said, 'we will fight as you direct us.'[6] This set the tone for his preferred model of leadership—being the sole person in charge. He was not one for democratic consultation.

His early experience in London as a member of the Executive Committee of the Vegetarian Society must have taught him, at that early stage, how to draft petitions, and how to convince someone hostile of the justice of your cause. Vegetarians were a minority, and decent though they might have been, they were treated as strange creatures by their fellow British. That was a lot like how Indian immigrants were treated in Natal. He knew how to plead his case, not just as a barrister, but also as someone who believed in the cause he was pleading.

It was in South Africa that he discovered that bargaining from an inferior position in a racist country, he could not just pursue a Constitutionalist path. So he evolved a way of making the number of his supporters count. His own experience on the way to Pretoria from Durban via Petermaritzberg taught him that the adversary had superior force, which he could employ without English scruples about the rule of law.

His experience in Natal, defending the conditions of Asian immigrants, required him to fight the hard attitudes of the British

[6]Gandhi, M.K., *An Autobiography: or the Story of My Experiments with Truth*, Mahadev Desai (trans.), Navjivan, Ahmedabad, 1927/2004, p. 129.

■ 12 ■

colonists in power there. He took his appeal to London as he had much faith in the promise made in Victoria's declaration to treat her Indian subjects equally with all her other subjects, although this did not always help. But he did get a taste for the practice of representing his case to British ministers in London.

While he was in Natal, the second war broke out between the Boers and the British (1899–1902), which spread across South Africa to Natal. This was driven by the discoveries of gold in Transvaal territory, and diamonds just to the north where Cecil Rhodes had established the colony which came to bear his name—Rhodesia (now Zimbabwe). Despite his dispute with the Natal government, MKG offered to recruit an ambulance corps from among the Indian immigrants to help the wounded soldiers. Thus he demonstrated a complex approach to the British, as well as his Indian followers, that while he opposed some of the laws in Natal, he was a loyal subject of the British Empire. This complexity became his unique characteristic—all the more so as he emphasized his nonviolent approach in the struggle over the rights of immigrants.

The Boer War had still not ended when Gandhi returned to India. After a fierce set of battles, the British established their mastery over the Boer settlements. The Union of South Africa was formed in 1902 with four provinces—Cape, Natal (both British-dominated), Transvaal and the Orange Free State (both with a Boer majority). The British were in overall control, but the Boers had proved that they were not easy to subdue.

Asian immigrants living in the Transvaal recalled Mohandas Gandhi from India once more in 1902. This was because Joseph Chamberlain, the cabinet minister of the British government, who had been prominent during the Boer War, was coming to

South Africa, and the positions of White British settlers and Asian immigrants were to be decided in the newly established Republic. So Mohandas moved to Johannesburg (Durban was his previous abode). He found that the Boers were even more rabidly anti-Asian than the British colonists of Natal. So the tactics he used in Natal were not enough. Passive but mass resistance became his innovation in political agitation. He innovated the satyagraha.

Again, he had to launch a struggle against discriminatory legislation for immigrants. He launched his satyagraha appealing to Indians—Hindus and Muslims, Gujarati-, Urdu- and Tamil-speaking immigrants, Chinese workers, men and women including his wife and sons, to go to prison in large numbers to defy the unjust laws. This struggle was launched in 1906, and one way or another, occupied him till 1914. As the relevant minister on the Transvaal side, Jan Smuts proved to be a tough negotiator. Smuts had been a brilliant student at Cambridge, and like Gandhi, he was a barrister and practised in Johannesburg. He was just two years younger than Gandhi, and was appointed attorney general of Transvaal at 27. His hands were tied by the Parliament (Raad) of Transvaal, which had the uncompromising Boers refusing to show any toleration towards the migrants. Gandhi got some concession, but, as we well know, apartheid remained in South Africa through much of the twentieth century. Gandhi contributed by example, which informed Black Africans as well as Black African-Americans. His name became well known, not just in India, but around the world. When he returned to India in late 1914, he was just 45 and was called 'Mahatma'.

So what did he learn from his experiments in South Africa? He tried to use the status of Indians as subjects within Victoria's

Empire as a promise that they must be granted equal status with other imperial subjects all over the Empire. Victoria's Declaration upon taking over the command of India promised her Indian subjects that they would be treated like all her other subjects without discrimination. But even more than that, his own experience of England and the English he met there was so good that he developed a deep appreciation for English decency and their sense of justice. All his life, this never left him. He did not immediately see that it was a peculiar form of Empire-loyalism to privilege Indian indentured labourers and merchants above native Africans. But it took him some years of living in South Africa, especially as he moved from Natal to the Transvaal, from a British- to a Boer-ruled part of South Africa to realize the futility of this stance. The demand for special treatment for Indians as Victoria's subjects, with a guarantee for equal treatment with respect to her other subjects, did not work in Boer South Africa; but his loyalty to the Empire was reflected, as was his English experience, in him expecting the White rulers in South Africa to play the games of power as they would play cricket. Though he got to know Black Africans and their struggles, he did not know enough to couple together Indians and Africans in their struggle against the White races. Even so, his admiration for the English was unbounded. As he said in a debate in Johannesburg in 1908, 'it was the Mission of the English race, even when they are subject races, to raise them [Indians and Africans], to equality with themselves, to give them absolutely free institutions and make them absolutely free men.'[7]

---

[7]Guha, Ramachandra, *Gandhi Before India*, Penguin Random House, Gurgaon, 2013, p. 293.

Muhammad Ali Jinnah 1896-1914

Muhammad found, upon returning to India after a period of unemployment, that opportunities opened up in the legal world of Bombay through contacts with British men. After all, Bombay was his home before he went to London, as his father had moved the family from Karachi (the dates are uncertain). So he was back home. Indeed, all his life, he treated Bombay as his hometown, living later in a fine house on Malabar Hill. Indeed, some later reports in 1947 said that he wanted to spend his weekends in Bombay, even after the Partition! Very soon, he was offered a temporary job as a presidency magistrate, and after that his path was smooth. He was successful as an excellent pleader of cases, and became well paid quite soon.

There are queries which we can wonder about. Could Mohan have done this had he patiently spent time in Bombay, even though he lacked clients? Was it having a family with children, and his brothers expecting some payback for the debt incurred in sending him to London, which pushed Mohan to South Africa? Would Mohan have taken to politics had he established a successful career as a barrister?

Muhammad reached a respectable status early in his life. His practice thrived. In the early days, he was the sole Muslim barrister. Soon, he started earning enough money to buy a carriage, move to a better apartment, and bring his young sister Fatema to live with him and go to a convent school in Bandra, a suburb of Bombay. Offered a job at ₹1,500 a month, he turned it down saying that he hoped to make that much in a day! He joined the Congress when he was just 30 years old. Given that at that time the Congress was a small gathering (not yet a political party) with fewer than a thousand members, the fact that he was admitted shows that he had achieved a status to be noticed, which was a difficult thing, especially in Bombay. There, he met leaders like Gokhale (a fellow Liberal) and Tilak (whose case he pleaded). He was a Moderate when the split occurred in the Congress on the occasion of the Partition of Bengal. Revolutionaries such as Aurobindo Ghosh used Hinduism as a weapon for recruitment. Muhammad stayed with Moderate Congressmen like Dadabhai Naoroji. He became a regular at Congress conferences. He was a rare Muslim in the Congress, as out of 706 members in 1896, only 17 were Muslim. This was not surprising since the Congress, at that time, consisted of the professional elite—rich lawyers, ex-civil servants, England-returned barristers—who were Hindus, Parsees and Christians. Few Muslims had trodden that path.

Being a rare Muslim in the Congress, Muhammad, in turn, attracted the attention of the Muslims. He did not join the Muslim League till 1913, seven years after he joined the Congress. But he appealed to the Muslim League to cooperate with the Congress by meeting at the same city and on the same date as the latter. This became a normal practice. Muhammad began to persuade Muslims and Hindus to unite on a common platform of fighting for self-government, but in a gradual, constitutional manner. He was not on the side of the Extremists who employed violent means after the Partition of Bengal in 1905. They also brought religion into politics, which was not to his liking (which may surprise many). In modern parlance, Muhammad was a secular constitutionalist.

Mohan might have missed the chance of becoming a big Bombay barrister, but his stay in South Africa rescued him from obscurity. The plight of Indian labourers in Natal became a talking point in India. At the age of 33, Muhammad was elected to the Imperial Legislative Council (a Parliament in embryo)—recently expanded to include elected representatives of Hindus and Muslims. Thus, he was able to argue the case of Indian immigrants in his speech there on 25 February 1910. Lord Hardinge, the viceroy presiding over it, objected to Muhammad's description of their treatment as cruel, but the latter did not withdraw it. This was the first significant, though somewhat remote, connection between Mohan and Muhammad.

Another connection was their friendship with, or even pupilage to, Gokhale—the senior Indian Liberal leader in the Congress. Muhammad admired Gokhale, and they went on a tour of Europe together in 1913. Mohan also acknowledged Gokhale as his mentor. He was able to get Gokhale to come to South Africa during his final struggle with Smuts to modify the severe conditions to be imposed on Asians in the Transvaal. Gokhale believed that he was promised a concession by Smuts regarding the £3 tax on Asians, but that proved to be not quite deliverable. Gokhale's power worked with British imperialism in India, but in the Transvaal, there was the extra dimension of Boer racism.

Even so, Gokhale was a guide to MKG when he returned to India. Indeed, he planned to meet up with Gokhale in London on his way back to India from South Africa. But the war had started by then. Gokhale was held up in France. They met in London in early 1915. Gokhale died in February 1915, soon after Mohan's return in January 1915. It was a great loss for both Mohan and Muhammad.

How South Africa Made Mohandas Karamchand Gandhi into a Mahatma

Mohandas became famous early on in his life. Indeed, it could be argued that he was the first Indian of his generation to be known abroad before he was known in India. This is thanks to his biography by Reverend Joseph Doke, titled *M.K.Gandhi: An Indian Patriot in South Africa,* published as early as 1909 when Mohandas was just 40. Joseph Doke was an English Baptist preacher from Devon. He first saw Mohandas when the latter was recovering from an assault perpetrated on him by some Pathans who were clearly not enamoured of passive resistance. Doke made his acquaintance, and became a friend. He was the first person in whom Mohandas confided the stories of his childhood in India. To some extent, the story as reported by Doke differs from the story Gandhi told in his autobiography written 15 years later, as we shall see. Mohandas saw to it that this biography was made available when he visited London in 1909 to argue the case for Indian immigrants in South Africa before the imperial government in London. Mohandas was quite savvy with spreading his name and his message all his adult life.

The year 1909 was also when Mohan met, during his visit to London, a young Indian training like him to be a barrister. Vinayak Damodar Savarkar was a staunch Hindu nationalist, who was to have a lifetime of disagreement with Mohandas Gandhi about Hinduism and its message, as well as other matters. Savarkar wanted India to be modern and industrialized after Independence. Mohandas was, by then, convinced that modernization, especially along Western lines, was evil. India, when independent, would have to reject that path. He wrote his first book *Hind Swaraj* on his way back from London to South Africa, on board the steamship.

(He obviously failed to see the irony inherent in penning such a critique while travelling on a posh luxury ship made possible only by the hated Western technology!)

Mohandas grew up to full manhood in South Africa and became what came to fruition in India—a Mahatma. Crucially, he was alone, away from his brothers and sister, and, for some of the time, even his wife and young sons. He sought guidance from the few individuals he treated as worth asking, such as Raychandbhai, a Jain man who was like a monk, to clear up the doubts he had about spiritual matters. But in his splendid isolation, he developed his own certainties. He worked out his version of Hinduism which was shaped by his family's Gujarati Vaishnavite faith (Vaishnavism differs across India depending on the region), Jain as well as Muslim influences, and the peculiar concoction of Christianity—an amalgam of esoteric Christianity and Methodism—which he had developed himself after talking to and reading the books of some friends he had made in England.

It must be remembered that during the years Mohan was in England and South Africa—the final years of the Victorian Era—there was an energetic debate in England challenging the official Anglican Church, Darwin having cast doubts on the story of Genesis, and non-denominational Churches such as Methodism spreading and growing in appeal. Socialism was in the air. The Boer War, which happened during his stay in South Africa, shook his confidence in the British and their superiority. There was a Suffragette campaign gathering momentum. Mohan saw the weakening of the British Empire first-hand, though these were still early days.

What was striking was his immense sense of self. It was not egoism, but a conviction that he was somehow the unique judge of Right and Wrong, not just for himself, but also for everyone around him. I quoted his own statement above as to how he approached Sir Edward Arnold about setting up a Vegetarian Club in Bayswater. This sort of confidence would have been rare in a 19-year-old Hindu boy who had just moved abroad. Where did he get this confidence from?

There is only one signal for this which his autobiography provides from his childhood. Since *SMET* was written after his return from Africa, it is interesting to note what he said there. This was when he wrote about his father dying. He was the one regular and constant nurse by his father's bedside. But then an uncle arrived to look after Karamchand. This would indicate that the uncle had learnt about the seriousness of the patient. In a well-known passage, Mohan recalled how, following a long day of nursing his father, his uncle offered to take his place, and Mohan then got into bed with his young wife. Soon, there was a knock on the door, and he heard that his father was no more. His reaction was striking. He wrote more than 30 years after the event: 'I should have been massaging him and then he would have died in my arms. But now my uncle had this privilege.'[8]

This simple observation was followed by him castigating his own behaviour in going off to bed as proof of his eager sexuality. This has been often cited. But the interesting bit is that he obviously missed the *privilege* of having his father die in his arms. Being the youngest son, he must have been special to have been asked to nurse his father. Or so at least he seemed to have thought. Hence, it had to be his privilege which now somehow

---

[8]Gandhi, M.K., *An Autobiography: or The Story of My Experiments with Truth*, Mahadev Desai (trans.), Navjivan, Ahmedabad, 1927/2004, p. 28.

went to his uncle. He did not fault his uncle, but blamed his own eagerness to be with his young wife. But the way it happened was quite normal. He had been nursing his father all day. His uncle was being helpful in taking over from him at night. This would be normal in any household. Neither him being replaced nor his father dying were abnormal events demanding an explanation. He did not even say how sad he was that his father had died. It was his idea of the *privilege* to be at his father's side which tells us how special he thought he was as the son of Karamchand. There was a sense of entitlement thwarted.

When he recounted his childhood to Rev. Doke in South Africa, he did not mention this. By 1924, he had sublimated himself from his slavery to the senses, and was pursuing *brahmacharya*. It could be that he saw this as castigating his sexuality for the loss in retrospect. But the giveaway word is *privilege*.

He was quite a dictator to his wife and sons. But that was par for the course in Indian households then. He was obsessive about his sexuality, and hence went on his quest for brahmacharya (celibacy) after the birth of his third son (their fourth child, as their firstborn daughter died young), but he did not mention consulting his wife in *SMET*. Of course, by that age, after 30-odd years of having an active sex life, the ardent desire for sex wears off naturally for most couples. But few make a philosophy out of it, and advertise it as a universal cure. But he was on his own with no one else to challenge him spiritually or rationally. Whether it be the strategy of how to fight against some new piece of troublesome legislation, or taking the initiative to march off to London to lobby the Cabinet, it was always MKG who was acknowledged as the sole leader. So he got used to parleying with heads of government in South Africa, such as Lord Milner, or Cabinet ministers in London quite early on in his life. He began laying down rules for diet, healthcare, and sexual abstinence for families who were to reside in his settlements—the Phoenix and Tolstoy farms. This habit of laying down the law as to how to behave stayed with him, and was extended to a nationwide audience once he got back to India as a Mahatma.

His first protest against Boer authorities in the Transvaal was the original seed from which satyagraha blossomed. Let us not forget that Mohandas Gandhi was not even 40 yet in September 1906 when he launched his first satyagraha. It was here that he mentioned *hartal*, a practice whereby Indian shopkeepers and other commercial enterprises stayed shut. Being related to the bazaar, it was a tactic that was familiar to the ordinary Indian. By trying it out first in Johannesburg in September 1906, he was putting it through a tougher test than he would experience in India since the Boers, as he knew by now, were more racist than the British in Natal, not to mention back home in London.

As he wrote in his *Indian Opinion* at the time,

When we are dissatisfied with anything, we resort to hartal. In India, we often consider it our duty to do so, in order to obtain redress of our grievances, particularly in the Native States. The *hartal* only means that we do not approve of a certain measure taken by the ruler. This tradition of resisting a law has been in vogue among us from very early days, when the English people were in a barbarous State.[9]

---

[9]Guha, Ramachandra, *Gandhi Before India*, Penguin Random House, Gurgaon, 2013, p. 209.

But as far as his campaigns were concerned, it cannot be said that he was successful. The ruling powers in South Africa were not to be overruled by the Colonial Office or anyone else in London. They had proved as much to the imperial power in the Boer War. What South Africa gave him was the status of 'the Sole Spokesman'[10] (to use an expression famously used about MAJ) of the Indians in South Africa. He was negotiating one-to-one with the top leaders. He had been able to travel to London to argue the brief for his people with ministers like Joseph Chamberlain and Winston Churchill, and with Jan Smuts in South Africa. Smuts was one opponent who was just as tough in bargaining as Mohandas Gandhi could be. The latter tried to get London to tell Pretoria what to do, but Pretoria would not listen. The discrimination against Indians did not cease, Queen Victoria's Declaration notwithstanding. We know it took just about a hundred years after Mohan's arrival in Durban for the Black Africans and Indians in South Africa to defeat Apartheid. When Mohan tried to do so during the 20 years or more that he spent there, White Africa did not surrender to his demands. But the experience taught him how to get to the top for a one-on-one negotiation. Patient petitioning from the back benches of a Parliament was not his style.

However, he became better known in India. He took care to keep the Congress informed of his campaigns. He even had hopes that the government of India may twist the arm of their White counterparts in South Africa to get justice for *their* Indian subjects. But no such luck. What Mohandas did achieve was full maturity in his spiritual search for a political philosophy which

---

[10]Jalal, Ayesha, *The Sole Spokesman: Jinnah, the Muslim League and the Demand for Pakistan*, Cambridge University Press, New Delhi, 1985.

was completely unique. South Africa was just a laboratory. The experiment—not so much with Truth, but political tactics—would be tried under better, though not perfect, conditions in India.

TWO

FROM SHADOWS TO THE CENTRE STAGE

In 1915, when MKG finally returned to India, he was 45, while MAJ was just 40. But as barristers, MAJ was much more of a success than MKG. In their political activities, in India for MAJ and South Africa for MKG, respectively, MAJ was building a high-flying career. MKG had garnered a lot of admiration in India for his work in South Africa, but he had not yet reached the heights that he, or anyone else, could ever have anticipated. Obviously much more has been written about MKG than MAJ. Despite being involved in active politics much of their adult lives, there is a disproportionality in the literature available about the two. MAJ was very much a private man. He seldom talked about himself, even in the context of politics. He did not leave a memoir or encourage writings about himself. His married life was brief, tragic in a way, but remains a guarded secret. He remains an enigma. By concentrating on his political agenda in the last 15 years of his life (after returning from London a second time), he appeared to be a soulless, humourless, fanatical person, which he definitely was not. He was, of course, widowed, and his daughter was not with him. Apart from his sister Fatema, he had no friends, just followers or fellow politicians with whom he had to struggle to win arguments. So the problem of writing about MAJ is to rescue him from his own silence, while, at the same time, filtering out much of the hostile noise, to say nothing about the overblown Islamic accolades surrounding his public reputation in Pakistan.

The problem with writing about MKG is that he wrote so much about himself throughout his life that he crowds out anyone else who could imagine other explanations for why he did what he did. Through his life, he kept telling the world about his innermost thoughts, and how his failings, as he saw them, had consequences for his impact on the world at large. Rarely do we see such a constant engagement with one's inner feelings, even while discussing major political events, in any other political leader. He crowds out alternative narratives about his actions and motivations. Yet, it is possible to envisage various plausible explanations for understanding his behaviour. So the best way is to quote him as and when necessary, but then, not to take his word as the definitive explanation. No doubt, what he tells us is the truth, but it is the truth as he sees it. Truth is not unique. Life is more like *Rashomon*.

India 1900-14

Much had changed not only in India, but in the world, since MKG went to South Africa. He was, of course, aware of the Congress which had been meeting annually since 1885. Starting from a polite, fervently Empire-loyalist, and elitist gathering, the Congress had become politically noisier and assertive. Dadabhai Naoroji altered the expectations of Indians not only by winning a seat in the House of Commons, but also by inaugurating a critique of the economic benefits and costs of the Empire.

In the new century, two developments further stirred the

calm waters. First, the Muslim League was established in 1907 as a separate organization for advancing the interests of Muslims. The British blamed the Muslims for the 1857 uprising since the avowed intention of the uprising (regardless of what the later views say) was the restoration of Mughal rule in Delhi. Muslims suffered discrimination due to this in government jobs and other favours. Muslims knew Persian and Arabic, which were official languages under Muslim rule. The British moved to using English. Moreover, the community was also slow in taking to Western education which had been on offer for over 50 years by then. Having been the rulers in Delhi for 500 years or so, a sense of entitlement delayed the Muslims' realization that British power was here to stay, and they had to adapt to this reality as the Hindus had with alacrity. (Again, it is very important not to think of the year 1907 as only 40 years before Independence or the Partition. No one then could have imagined the end of the British Empire any time in their lifetimes.)

Sir Syed Ahmad Khan, who was knighted for his services to the Empire, realized that reforms were needed to raise the economic and social standing of Muslims. He wanted Muslims to demonstrate their loyalty to the Crown, take to Western education, and modernize their ways. It was to this effect that the Muslim League was formed in the first decade of the new century. Like the Congress, it was established by the elite but, in the Muslim case, it was mainly minor princes and substantial landlords from North India who were the leaders of the League. To use modern parlance, the Muslim bourgeoisie was rather small compared to the Hindu and Parsee bourgeoisie.

Early on in the new century, Muslims were cheered by the

decision of Viceroy Lord Curzon to partition Bengal in 1905. Of course, what was called Bengal then comprised Bihar and Orissa as we know them now. Bengal, at that time, included what are now West Bengal and Bangladesh. Indeed, our story is about what happened to Bengal over the next half-century and more.

Curzon said that the partition was for administrative convenience. In a way, given how many provinces (as we now have) were combined in one, it was a convincing explanation for his point. But the mood in Bengal itself was not of that view. This was because, in fact, there was a de facto division of Bengal (proper) along the lines of community and class. Hindus lived mostly in West Bengal, but they were also the landlords across large tracts of land in East Bengal. The peasants in East Bengal were predominantly Muslim. Making East Bengal a separate province would empower Muslims as they would be the majority community.

There was an eruption among Bengali Hindus, which had a ferocity not seen in India since 1857. A movement gathered strength among young Hindu Bengalis to protest against the partition. It took a violent militant form. Muslims in East Bengal did not protest, but they were also largely poor and illiterate. The minority that understood what happened, such as the nawab of Dhaka, welcomed the partition.

The conventional historical view in (post-Independence) India greets the Bengal uprising as the start of the march towards Independence. The young revolutionaries adopted the poem 'Vande Mataram' (salute the motherland) from *Anandamath* (1882), a classic novel by Bankim Chandra Chatterjee, as their anthem. The novel focuses on the movement by an army of Hindu *sadhu*s (holy men) who fight against Muslim rule. Bankim meant it as a hidden criticism of British rule, but Muslims saw it differently. For one thing, the poem asked people to bow down to, i.e. worship, 'Mother' (India) which was bound to be against the Muslim faith and practice. But the poem also contained words which could be interpreted as a protest against the rulers whom Hindus have been fighting for centuries. The idea that Muslim rule was as foreign as the British became one pillar of the movement. The singing of 'Vande Mataram' at the annual conferences of the Congress became a matter of division.[11]

The Congress was split at the reaction of the youthful Bengalis who were also joined by some Punjabi- and Marathi-speaking youth. They took to the bomb and the gun. At its 1907 Surat Conference, tempers flared and the Congress expelled the 'Extremists'—among them Bal Gangadhar Tilak of Maharashtra, Lala Lajpat Rai of Punjab, and Bipin Chandra Pal of Bengal.

There was another development in that very first decade of the century, which was politically much more substantial as well as consequential. The Liberals came to power in London in 1905, and were to rule for the next 17 years, one way or another. The nascent Labour Party also won some seats. This was thanks to the efforts by leaders of the early trade unions which eventually became the Labour Party. The Liberal Party was friendly towards India and its aspirations. Ramsay MacDonald and Keir Hardie

---

[11]When Independence came in 1947, along with the Partition, the demand to make 'Vande Mataram' the National Anthem was overruled. Another Bengali poem written by Rabindranath Tagore, 'Jana Gana mana' (its first stanza), was chosen. In one of its later stanzas, the poem lists the people of India as comprising 'Hindu, Bauddha, Sikh, Jain, Parasik, Mussalman, Christani'—a much better characterization of India before or after Independence.

were among the Labour MPs who had sympathies for India. There was a growing willingness for granting some measure of consultative representation to Indians.

Curzon himself, while he was the undersecretary of state for India in the Conservative government of Marquess Salisbury, had, in 1892, added representatives of associations in business and civil society (as we would put it today) as members of the Legislative Council advising the viceroy. This had, however, not introduced any commercial or really representative element. The Morley-Minto Reforms of 1909 expanded the Imperial Legislative Council to include 28 elected members, compared to the 16 added in the 1892 proposals. The seats were divided among Hindus and Muslims, with a 30 per cent share for Muslims.

There is a popular Indian belief that the British practised a policy of 'divide-and-rule'. But the divisions existed between Hindus and Muslims long before the British came into the picture. As Maulana Mohammad Ali said (perhaps quoting Gandhi), 'We Divide, They Rule'. What was new was the franchise and elections as a way of selecting who would represent Indians in the Advisory Council. As things stood, the franchise was not universal yet— even in the UK. The British took the view for their own society, as for any other, that every society had separate groups defined by religion and region, not to mention class. Ireland was there as a ready example—a nation divided between Catholics and Protestants. England itself had progressed slowly, recognizing the rights of Catholics, Methodists and Jews over the course of the nineteenth century. So it was natural, or even obvious, for them to see that there were communities in India which were distinct. Since 1871, the census of India counted the population according to their religious affiliations. Indeed, words such as 'Hindu' and 'Hinduism' only came into use then. Otherwise, the religion had no name except 'Sanatan Dharma' (the Perennial Order). 'Hindu' is not a Sanskrit word, but a Persian one, derived from 'Sindhu', the river Indus.

The franchise was limited by the level of income, which was similar to what British voters had. A concession was made that the qualifying income level was higher for Hindus than it was for Muslims. But this was fair as Muslims had lower incomes than Hindus as a group. The Congress did not like the Morley-Minto Reforms, as was its well-known *modus operandi*, but eventually it did accept the half-loaf it was getting. But in later accounts of the Partition, the Morley-Minto Reforms loom large as the original poisoned apple of divide-and-rule offered by the imperialists to the innocent people of the subcontinent. It is always easy to blame the outsider.

Jinnah immediately saw the seriousness of the issue. He was, after all, sufficiently persuaded by the Liberals during his stay in England to become a Liberal Constitutionalist. He began his campaign to work towards Hindu-Muslim unity by persuading the Muslim League that it should coordinate its annual conference to be held in the same location and on the same date as that of the Congress. He wanted the Congress (as a de facto Hindu or, at least, a non-Muslim organization) to accommodate the Muslim demand. He spent most of the decade after 1909 working on this, and succeeded in getting an agreement at the Lucknow Conference in 1916. Alas, the world changed drastically soon afterwards. One of the ways in which it changed had to do with MKG and his unique approach to politics. Let us, therefore, turn to MKG.

Gandhi Back in India (1915–25)

One thing MKG made clear even before he departed from London (where he had arrived with his family from South Africa, on his way back to India) was his determination to prove his loyalty to the Empire. The Great War (not yet known as the First World War at that time) had started, and he wanted to recruit Indians of his acquaintance as volunteers in an ambulance team as he had done in South Africa. He continued to appeal for recruitment in the Imperial Army on his return to India.[12] This was something in which MAJ refused to join him. Loyal though MAJ was, he was unwilling to go the lengths that MKG went. The latter was decorated with the Kaiser-I-Hind medal for his help in recruiting soldiers (he returned the medal as a protest against the Jallianwala Bagh Massacre in April 1919).

The next step MKG took was to try to meet up with Gokhale in London itself. Gokhale was his mentor and, as we saw previously, had assisted Mohan in his final struggle with Smuts in South Africa. But it was unusual for Gokhale to extend help so directly. He was of the constitutionalist branch of the Congress. Gokhale's willingness to use his position to help MKG showed the high regard he had for the latter. The question facing MKG was how he was going to enter Indian politics. He was eager to be active in the Congress. He had been attending its annual conferences whenever he happened to be in India on short breaks from South Africa. But now, he had to find a way to get in and make his mark.

MKG was known well enough in Indian political circles. Ten days after he arrived in London, Sarojini Naidu gave a reception

---

[12]Hunt, James D., *Gandhi in London*, Promilla Books, New Delhi, 2012.

for him at Hotel Cecil (which was MKG's usual abode when he came to London to argue his South African case with the Colonial Office). MAJ was present at this reception on 16 August 1914. This must have been the first face-to-face meeting between the two. Each had earned the distinction of being young politicians, and both were Gujarati. They met in Ahmedabad next, at a meeting organized by the Gurjar Sabha. K.M. Munshi, a lawyer, a great creative writer in Gujarati and Congress member, was the host. It was a moot question as to who was the better-known Gujarati. Jinnah was known as the member of the Central Legislative Assembly. Gandhi had already been described as Mahatma since his return to India.

In retrospect, this may seem an outrageous question. How many think of Jinnah as a Gujarati, especially since he seldom spoke the language in public? But as of that date in 1915, chances are that Jinnah was being looked upon with admiration while Gandhi was just getting to be known face-to-face in Gujarat. Jinnah obviously did it the right way. He came back to India from England, spent a couple of years pounding the streets of Bombay, but built up his career in law through sheer persistence. He joined the Congress in 1906 when he was just 30, but also did enough for Muslims to be chosen to represent them in the Imperial Legislative Council. Indeed, by 1915, he was in his second term.

Gokhale, who knew them both, asked MKG to get to know India properly before plunging into politics. So Mohandas chose to travel around India by rail. Unlike most Indian political leaders, especially those who were England-returned, and dressed in the English style (MAJ was a stylish dresser in the English style all his life), Mohandas had already changed his attire from the style of an English barrister to simple Indian outfits. It was, as yet, a middle-class Gujarati attire, not that of the poor peasant, which he adopted soon after. It was not unusual for politicians to dress in the Indian style, but they dressed in upper-class clothes. MKG took Gokhale's advice seriously, and travelled around India from Madras and Sind to Burma (which was still regarded as a part of British India). He explored Gujarat, of course, and went to see Tagore at Shantiniketan.

Having moved around India as advised by his mentor, MKG made his first foray in Indian public life. Yet, sure as he was of himself, he managed to put a wrong foot forward in his first public engagement. It was at a gathering in Banaras on 4 February 1916, where Annie Besant (whom he had met in London long ago) founded a Hindu college. It was a great day for the Hindu College (later the Benares Hindu University). Viceroy Lord Hardinge was there, as were many kings and princes, as well as loyal Indians some of whom belonged to the Congress. The Maharaja of Darbhanga was presiding over it. Speaking at the gathering, MKG acted his own confident and superior self. He castigated previous speakers for not having spoken in Hindi, said how filthy Banaras was, criticized how luxuriously the various guests there were dressed, and how Indians would have to change their habits if they were to win concessions from the British, implying that he knew these things better than they did. This offended most people who were present, and Dr Annie Besant immediately took against him. This made an easy entry into the Congress difficult for him.

It was MAJ who seemed to have got MKG to sit on the platform at the 1916 meeting of the Congress, along with Annie Besant. It was a first time when responding to an appeal from

MAJ, the Muslim League arranged to meet in the same city as the Congress at the same time.

MAJ was then trying to get the two organizations together to agree on the arrangement of sharing the legislature seats promised in the reforms proposed by Morley and Minto. There were separate electorates, but MAJ wanted the two apex organizations of the two communities to agree on a formula for sharing. He roped in MKG to appear on the platform with him.

At the Lucknow Conference in 1916, MAJ achieved his cherished goal of getting an agreement from the Congress about the Muslim share of the seats in the separate electorate system. The numbers were in proportion to the Muslim population of the provinces—50 per cent in Punjab, 30 per cent in UP, 40 per cent in Bengal, 25 per cent in Bihar, 15 per cent in the Central Provinces, 15 per cent in Madras, 33 per cent in Bombay. This achievement made Sarojini Naidu describe MAJ as the 'Ambassador of Hindu-Muslim Unity'.

It is the task of the remaining chapters to explain how and why MAJ changed from Lucknow 1916 to Delhi 1946, and became the architect of Pakistan. The key to understanding this is his Gujarati compatriot MKG.

MKG in Action

After his Banaras experience, MKG changed tack. He founded an ashram in Ahmedabad which was the largest city in Gujarat as well as a centre of industry housing rich Gujarati businessmen. He was known well enough to receive generous donations from local businessmen. His field of action was then away from Congress conferences. He was asked, given his reputation as a champion for the interests of indentured workers, to come to Champaran in Bihar, and relieve the misery of indigo-growers there. This was a godsend because his tactic of peaceful mass protests against a recognizable, powerful opponent would work in this case. Here, he was not confronting a racist regime, but prosperous indigo farmers many of whom were British. He took recourse to the law to organize petitions and protests. He attracted the attention of a young Bihari lawyer Rajendra Prasad (many years later, he would be independent India's first president) and a teacher J.B. Kripalani, who were inspired by his presence, and became his life-long followers. MKG ended the episode with credit. He gathered evidence from the farmers cultivating indigo about the taxes and deductions they had to face, and placed them before a committee appointed by the Bihar government. The farmers' case was recognized, and relief was offered to them. The details need not concern us here. In any case, they have been well described in his biographies. But what is less known or forgotten is that to reinforce his imperial loyalty record, he said of his victory: 'In Champaran by resisting an age-long tyranny, I have shown the ultimate sovereignty of British justice.'[13]

The other opportunity for applying his tactic was in Ahmedabad itself, where cotton mill workers were involved in a wage dispute. Here again, his charisma attracted followers, one of whom was the sister of a big mill-owner, who also happened to have financially supported the ashram. MKG went on a fast to persuade the two sides to come to an agreement. This was a complete innovation on his part. Fasting is a part of the religious

---

[13]Saiyid, Matlubul Hasan, *Jinnah: A Political Study*, Shaikh Muhammad, Lahore, 1945, p. 170.

practice in Hinduism. But no one used it as a tactic in settling industrial disputes. Gandhi's reputation, his persona, and the fact that he was completely at home in Ahmedabad culturally worked like magic. No one wanted to see this thin man in simple garments, emaciated as he was, come to any harm.

What Gandhi had done was demonstrate, safely away from the annual meetings of the Congress where the approach was constitutionalist and gradual, the efficacy of his innovative techniques of settling problems. He was also reaching much of India, which the Congress had not. In South Africa, whatever he may have thought, such religiously saturated tactics cut no ice. But in India, the cultural context was like the air the people breathed. A fast by a 'great man'—a Mahatma—had an electric effect. Gandhi found his niche. He would be able to play his religiosity to the full extent as a weapon for effecting political action in India. Soon, he did not need the Congress. It needed him.

Soon after his return, in a letter to *The Statesman* based out of Calcutta, he wrote:

> Rightly or wrongly, the worship of the cow is ingrained in the Hindu nature and I see no escape from a most bigoted and sanguinary strife over this question between Christians and Muslims on the one hand and Hindus on the other. But there is not a Hindu throughout the length and breadth of India who does not expect one day to free his land from cow-slaughter. But contrary to the genius of Hinduism as I know it, he would not mind forcing even at the point of the sword either the Christian or the Mohammedans to abandon cow-slaughter.[14]

---

[14]Ibid., 165.

This was an affirmation of his Hindu credentials, which was, as one would say now, a bit over the top. But *The Statesman* was widely read by the English in India as well as Indians, who were their chosen elite. But MKG was never a simple person to analyze. He had been associating with Muslims—many of them Gujarati-speaking—in South Africa. As he said in *SMET*, he had a Muslim friend in his schooldays. So in October 1916, when there was a Gujarat Provincial Conference in Ahmedabad, it was MKG who had the pleasant task of proposing the name of MAJ as the president of the gathering. MKG said of MAJ: 'a learned Muslim of our times' and 'a person who holds [a] respected position in the eyes of both parties.'[15]

At this time, MAJ was concentrating on Hindu-Muslim unity. Thus, at that provincial conference, MAJ said:

> There is but one question beside the question of Cow-killing and street music, which has proved not only a thorny question, but an obstacle, which has kept the two communities hitherto apart. But the solution is not difficult. It requires the spirit of conciliation, and, give and take. The Muslims want proper, adequate and effective representation in the Council chambers of the country, and in the District and Municipal Boards, a claim which no right-minded Hindu disputes for a moment. But the Muslims further require that representation in the various Boards and Council chambers be secured to them by means of separate electorates. This question of separate electorates from top to bottom has been before the country ever since 1909, and, rightly or wrongly,

---

[15]Guha, Ramachandra, *Gandhi: The Years that Changed the World: 1914–1918*, Penguin Random House, Gurgaon, 2018, p. 37.

the Muslim community is absolutely determined for the present to insist on separate electorates... The demands for separate electorates is not a matter of policy, but a matter of necessity... I would therefore appeal to my Hindu brethren that, in the present state of position, they should try to win the confidence and the trust of the Muslims who are, after all, in the minority in the country. If they are determined to have separate electorates, no resistance should be shown to their demand.

Hindus and Muslims united and firm, the voice of three hundred million people vibrating throughout the length and breadth of the country, will produce a force which no power on earth can resist.[16]

So the two young Gujaratis—who were also proud of being English barristers—were striking out together. Jinnah, no doubt, was well known through his work, and the high status he had achieved as a parliamentarian. It was hard to say who was the better known. But MKG could not resist insisting when he got a chance that Indian leaders should talk in their local language, if they could. This was what he had said at Banaras in his first public engagement in India since his return. Now when he got a chance, he did the same at another Gujarat Political Conference in November 1917, where Tilak and Jinnah were invited. Asked to speak in Gujarati by MKG, MAJ 'made a brave show of stammering out his speech in Gujarati.'[17]

[16]Saiyid, Matlubul Hasan, *Jinnah: A Political Study*, Shaikh Muhammad, Lahore, 1945, p. 126.
[17]Guha, Ramachandra, *Gandhi: The Years that Changed the World: 1914–1918*, Penguin Random House, Gurgaon, 2018, p. 51.

MKG had this bee in his bonnet that Indian political leaders should speak in their local languages. At Banaras, he admonished people so that they would speak in Hindi. He could not let go of a chance to persuade MAJ to speak in Gujarati. Jinnah had never been recorded to be speaking in Gujarati apart from this one occasion mentioned above. But MKG kept up his campaign. Thus there is a letter to MAJ who was sailing off to London with his wife Ruttie (Rattanbai). He wrote on 28 June 1919:

> Dear Mr. Jinnah,
>
> And, of course, I have your promise that you will take up Gujarati and Hindi as quickly as possible. May I then suggest that like Macaulay you learn one of these languages on your return voyage?

This admonition also seems to have fallen on infertile ground. Many years later, MKG wrote to a friend that Jinnah had hated him since the day he asked him in a meeting 'to give up English and speak in Gujarati'.[18]

All Change

Then suddenly, three things happened which totally changed the context of British-Indian relations. The Great War had been going on in Europe, and lasted longer than any of the belligerents had expected. It also consumed a much larger quantity of manpower in the field, and was much more destructive than anyone had thought likely. India emerged as a major source of soldiers fighting

---

[18]Ibid., 273.

for the Allies. The Indian Army had been trained to fight abroad in the Middle East, Africa and even as far as China. But this was the first time the British saw them in action near their home. The Indian Army made a difference. The Axis Powers had no comparable colony to source soldiers for fighting in the war.

Britain was going through several fundamental changes in its ancient Constitution. The large and convincing majority which the Liberals won in 1995 not only displaced their old rivals—the Conservative Party—but also brought in a few members of the nascent Labour Party. Lloyd George, a Welshman (a minority that was hitherto not prominent in politics), was the chancellor of the exchequer in 1910. His radical budget tried to create a modern welfare state financed by taxes on the wealthy, many of whom sat in the House of Lords, on Conservative benches. After repeated efforts by the House of Lords to reject the budget, and much constitutional to-and-fro, the decision was made that henceforth financial matters would be decided in the House of Commons. The House of Lords—hitherto the senior, more powerful House—had to yield to the democratic upsurge. There was now a full franchise encompassing all adult men above 21 years of age. There was also a franchise for women but restricted to those over 30 years.

The war did not go as well as expected for the British. Asquith, who was the leader of the Liberals and the prime minister, was thought to be not decisive enough to be a great wartime leader. So after a party revolt among the Liberals, a coalition government was formed to be in power in Britain, with Lloyd George as prime minister. India was given a seat in the Imperial War Cabinet, along with the White Commonwealth countries Canada, Australia and New Zealand; Britain was beginning to appreciate the Empire's inputs in its own defence in this war which was proving to be much tougher than anyone had anticipated. It was obvious to Edwin Montagu, a rare Jewish appointment to the post of secretary of state for India, that a further advance was needed upon the Morley-Minto Reforms to reward India for its efforts. The proposal Montagu put forward was an unexpected commitment that a process of reforms would begin, which would see as its goal a substantial degree of self-government by Indians. The ultimate date was unclear, but the promise was firm. Curzon, who had been a viceroy to India, and was now in the Coalition Cabinet, warned against too fast a move in granting self-government, but he did not insist in the Cabinet that Montagu change his stance.[19] As a first instalment, there would be elected members of provincial legislative assemblies who would be put in executive charge of government departments. These were to be 'soft' subjects—health, education, and such others (what nowadays would be called human development issues). Montagu promised to visit India, and confer with the new viceroy Lord Chelmsford to work out the details of the proposals.

When he visited India, it was clear to Montagu how much politically advanced the Indian elite was. Of course, one would expect him, as a Jew, to be conscious of prejudice. But he met MAJ, and noticed how clever he was. As he remarked after meeting Jinnah, '[He] is a very clever man. And it is, of course, an outrage that such a man should have no chance of running the affairs of his own country.' Other British officials also saw what drove MAJ. Montagu was told that the root of Jinnah's

[19]Mosley, Leonard, *Curzon: The End of an Epoch*, Readers Union, Longman Green & co., London, 1961, pp. 171–72.

activities was ambition. He believed that when Mrs Besant and Tilak disappeared, he would be the leader (of the Congress).

This proved to be a deep insight into Jinnah's character, but not very prescient as to his future. One of the reasons why MAJ did not succeed Tilak and Besant as leader was, of course, his fellow Gujarati MKG, and a little trouble in the Middle East. That is the story to which we must turn.

During the war, the Axis powers were joined by the Ottoman Empire. The Empire was the spiritual heart of Sunni Muslims, and the Sultan was the Caliph (Khalifa) resident in Istanbul. In the course of the war, the Ottoman Empire lost its possessions in the Balkans—provinces which became Serbia and Bosnia Herzegovina, and later, parts of Yugoslavia. The Allies, led by Britain, had prised off these regions. This increased resentment towards the British among the Indian Muslims.

It was clear by 1917 that the Allies would defeat the Ottoman Empire, and during the war, a secret treaty was signed between the British Foreign Office and the French Quai d'Orsay—the Sykes-Picot Agreement—which divided up for the future parts of the Ottoman Empire as the responsibility of either France or Britain. The communists newly in power in Russia published some of these secret treaties. There was the proposal that the Khilafat—the seat of the Khalifa—would move to Jerusalem, which was to be under British control. Indian Muslims were worried that their spiritual home had fought against the British, and also about what would happen to the Sunni *ummah* with the displacement of the Khalifa.[20] The Muslim desire for some

---

[20]Desai, Meghnad, *Rethinking Islamism: The Ideology of the New Terror*, I.B. Tauris, London, 2007.

security in any future arrangement for self-government in India was also fuelled by this anxiety.

The other major change was the introduction of religion, especially Hinduism, in the politics of the independence movement. It was not just the arrival of MKG in India, but also the efforts of Annie Besant who had made India her home. Theosophy had a lot of affinity with mystical Hinduism, and Annie Besant was that rare Theosophist who was politically active in the British Fabian Society, along with fighting the battle for humanism and population control with Charles Bradlaugh, MP. She founded the Home Rule League—which was somewhat rare for an Indian political movement—in Madras in South India. The idea of home rule was popular in Irish politics, and Annie Besant had some Irish blood in her. There was an uprising in Dublin over the Easter of 1916, which set in motion a longer struggle of the Irish Catholics to get independence from Great Britain. Its goal was home rule. The Liberal Party had already diverged on the issue of home rule for Ireland, with a section of MPs joining the Conservatives as the Unionist Party led by Joseph Chamberlain—MAJ's hero. Just when the Congress and the Muslim League were joining forces, Besant not only started another movement but also made it more radical and religious. Tilak also founded his own Home Rule League.

Annie Besant was jailed in 1917, but then released. Her incarceration aroused much sympathy, and she was elected president of the Congress for the 1917 Calcutta session. She declared in her presidential speech:

> Home Rule has become so intertwined with religion by the prayers offered up in the great Southern temples—sacred

places of pilgrimage and spreading from there to village temples and also being preached up and down the country by Sadhus and Sanyasins.[21]

As a biographer of Jinnah wrote:

At a time when the religious feelings of the Muslims had already been roused by the deterioration of the international situation in the Balkans, and the extremist sections of opinion, both among the Hindus and Muslims, were preaching the separatist doctrines, it was not prudent on the part of the promoters of the Home Rule movement to direct its activities into the channels of sectarianism.[22]

This, however, is somewhat premature. The explosive effects of religion in Indian politics were to arrive not yet but a few years later.

Soon after that presidency at Calcutta, MKG replaced Annie Besant as head of the Home Rule Movement, and renamed it the Swaraj League. His religion did not speak of temples, sadhus or sanyasis, but the practice of satyagraha. There was nothing as such to antagonize the Muslims. When MKG addressed the Muslim League at its 1918 session in Calcutta, he made his pro-Muslim credentials clear. He appealed for the release of Mohammad Ali and Shaukat Ali from Chindwara—a small town in Central India, where they were in internment for opposing the policy of the British Empire in the Middle East. He said:

---

[21]Saiyid, Matlubul Hasan, *Jinnah: A Political Study*, Shaikh Muhammad, Lahore, 1945, pp. 161–62.
[22]Ibid., pp. 162–63.

> I found that the Muslim demand was not only not against the Government, but that the British Prime Minister has admitted the justice of the Muslim demands. I felt therefore bound to render all the help I could in securing the due fulfilment of the Prime Minister's pledge.[23]

This was a subtle way of telling Lloyd George, the then British prime minister, that the treatment of the Ottoman Emperor was a sensitive issue for the Muslims of India. Gandhi kept a constant eye on British policy, not just from an Indian perspective, but almost in the way a British person would look at it. At this stage, no one knew that this issue was going to blow up sky high in India.

Though during his first few years back in India, there was a common endeavour on the parts of MAJ and MKG to pursue Hindu-Muslim unity, MAJ pursued it in terms of constitutional tactics while MKG went for broader considerations; the issue of Khilafat changed that. Ironically, this was because MKG championed Muslim religious interests, while MAJ thought these religious issues were irrelevant, if not dangerous.

But more was to change soon. The war brought about other changes. For one thing, inflation—unknown for the previous hundred years—became a problem for the middle classes. Soldiers who were injured began to return to India, and reported that they had seen how vulnerable the British looked in the early years of the war. Even in the Spring of 1918, few anticipated an end to the war, much less an Allied victory. So the recruitment of young soldiers continued in Punjab and the North-West—where the 'martial races' were supposed to live.

---

[23]Ibid.

The new viceroy Lord Chelmsford summoned political leaders to Delhi for a conference on recruitment campaigns in April 1918. MKG was keen to help. As he wrote to the viceroy:

> If I could make my countrymen retrace their steps, I would make them withdraw all the Congress Resolutions and not whisper Home Rule or Responsible Government during the pendency of the War. I would make India offer all the able-bodied sons as a sacrifice to the Empire at its critical moment.[24]

But he also told the viceroy that he should give 'definite assurances about Mohammedan states as every Mohammedan was deeply interested in them.' He surprised everyone when he chose to speak in Urdu at the conference. As Jinnah's biographer remarked, it was 'an ever memorable land-mark in Indian history.'[25] This was not his only memorable gesture. At the Muslim League Conference in December 1918 in Calcutta, he appealed to the viceroy to secure the release of the Ali brothers, Mohammad and Shaukat, who had been interned. 'With superb timing, MKG secured a victory over other Hindu leaders and, for the time being, he gained immeasurable support from the Muslims.'[26]

Gandhi was thus acting on many fronts. Some of his signals, such as asserting the Hindu desire for cow protection against likely assaults by Christians and Muslims, were orthodox pro-Hindu, but then, leaping to the defence of Muslim concerns shows his awareness of the global context in which Muslims viewed their

---

[24]Ibid., pp. 169–70.
[25]Ibid.
[26]Ibid.

political concerns. It was the ummah, not just India, which concerned the Indian Muslims. MKG had known many Muslims in South Africa, so he was aware of their sensitivities. Indeed, he had drafted a letter of felicitation to the Ottoman Sultan from the Muslims of Natal and Transvaal on his twenty-five years on the throne in 1900.

The difference between MKG and MAJ on the Hindu-Muslim issue began to become clear at this very early stage in their joint careers. Jinnah was only interested in the strictly political issue of the allocation of seats in keeping with the numerical size of the groups. That being accomplished at Lucknow, he did not dabble in any other issues such as cow slaughter. Gandhi had a totalizing vision, taking in religion, politics and everything else. This was one way in which he was not only unique, but also frustrating for many Congress or League members to understand.

THREE

FORKS IN THE ROAD TO FREEDOM

The major change made by Montagu's reform proposals was that while the Morley-Minto Reforms just expanded the size of the Imperial Legislative Council (i.e. at the Centre), Montagu opened up seats to be contested at provincial levels. The Lucknow Agreement had settled the allocation of seats from provinces to the Imperial Council where the total numbers were, in any case, small. Now with many provinces (some with a Muslim majority and others where Muslims were in a minority), the issue of seat allocation became central in Hindu-Muslim political relations. It opened up the possibility that as self-government took shape, India was most likely to be a federation. Then the question would be whether it would have a dominant or a weak Centre, and subordinate or autonomous provinces. A minority which had pockets of provinces where it was in a majority would prefer a weak Centre. The majority community at the national level would prefer a strong Centre. The controversy over Hindu-Muslim shares of seats had just become more intense. The Lucknow process needed to be opened up again.

But while London could propose, at the India end, events happened which totally upset the apple cart of the Empire. Soldiers had been going from Punjab and the North-West generally. Many of the injured were now coming back. In the middle of 1918, the government still felt that recruitment should be stepped up. (Again, with hindsight, we know that the war was over by November 1918. Why recruit in the middle of the year? Because those who were alive then did not know the war was going to be over.) There were still elements left over from the revolutionary tendencies that opened up in 1905, who were throwing bombs or plotting an army revolt. There was a lot of nervousness on the part of the government.

Lord Hardinge, the previous viceroy, narrowly escaped a bomb thrown at him while he was out in Delhi. Rash Behari Bose, a Bengali revolutionary, was trying to foment a rebellion in the Punjab Army. He was about to be caught, but managed to escape, and fled to Japan where he established a presence fighting the British from a distance. Twenty-odd years later, another Bengali revolutionary Subhas Chandra Bose sought his help in his campaign.

These developments worried the government of India. They appointed a committee chaired by Sir Sidney Rowlatt, a judge from England, with Kumaraswami Shastri and Provash Chandra Mitter as Indian members, to report on the measures to be taken 'to investigate and report on the nature and extent of the criminal conspiracies and to advise as to the legislation, if any necessary, to enable the Government to deal effectively with them.'

The committee's report raised a storm in the Imperial Legislative Council. Speaking critically, MAJ told the viceroy presiding over it that 'the first bomb was thrown in India after 1906, not before.' He argued cogently that the problem of the violent activities was created by the policies of the government of India since the partition of Bengal was proposed. The partition was reversed during the king emperor's visit in 1911, but the genie was out of the bottle. It was a new policy which was wanted.

The reversal of Bengal's partition and the transfer of the capital from Calcutta to Delhi have an interesting background. Lord Curzon, who initiated the partition, was not criticized for it at home. Indeed, his biographer Leonard Mosley barely mentions it. He resigned because he quarrelled with the commander-in-chief of the Indian Army—the newly appointed Lord Kitchener, the hero of Khartoum. The important decision to accompany the arrival of the king emperor—the only time an emperor did so in the long history of British India—required the capital to be shifted to Delhi, the seat of the Mughal Empire.[27]

Alas, no heed was taken of such complaints. The committee's report led to some proposed legislation which became the Rowlatt Acts. One act was 'to make provision in special circumstances to supplement ordinary criminal law and for the exercise of emergency powers by the Government.' Jinnah moved an amendment that the motion proposing the acts not be agreed to. But the amendment was lost. MAJ called the passage of Bills 1 and 2, and the viceroy's assent to put the measure on the Statute Book, 'a measure admittedly obnoxious and decidedly coercive at a time of peace thereby substituting the Executive for the Judiciary.' He resigned from the Imperial Legislative Council.

But now it was MKG who took the battle out of the Council Chambers, and employed his South African methods to the Indian problem. He called for a hartal which, as he already said, was a well-known Indian traditional practice of shutting shops as a form of protest. He tried this in South Africa in his 1906 campaign.

---

[27]Mosley, Leonard, *Curzon: The End of an Epoch*, Readers Union, Longman Green & co., London, 1961.

Suddenly, the context of the independence movement was radically changed. From polite constitutional debates, the protest was now in the daily bazaar. But he had not prepared his troops. The scale at which he was operating in India was much larger than that in Natal or the Transvaal. MKG had unchained a storm which, he found out soon, he could not contain. But he also proved to all and sundry that he had an appeal that was way beyond what the Congress managed in its 34 years of loyal speech-making. His appeal went out to all Indians:

> Being conscientiously of the opinion that the Bills known as the Indian Criminal Law (Amendment) Bill Number 1 of 1919 and the Criminal Law (Emergency Powers) Bill of 1919 are unjust, subversive of the principles of liberty and justice, and destructive of the elementary rights of individuals on which the safety of a community as a whole and the whole State itself is based, we solemnly affirm that, in the event of these Bills becoming law, and until they are withdrawn, we shall refuse civilly to obey these laws as a Committee to be hereafter appointed may think fit and we further affirm that in this struggle we will fruitfully follow truth and refrain from violence to life, person or property.[28]

MKG unleashed his weapon of open defiance of the law, where the person issuing the challenge announced his willingness to bear the punishment it entailed. It was a legal way of breaking the law. This was satyagraha coming home.

This was MKG's first experiment with satyagraha in India.

---

[28]Guha, Ramachandra, *Gandhi: The Years that Changed the World: 1914–1918*, Penguin Random House, Gurgaon, 2018.

But, as in his first foray in Banaras where he managed to surprise and offend, this time, too, he managed to start a riot. It may have been his lack of experience with India or even, unusually for him, an underestimation of his power to rouse the people. For one thing, when announcing the hartal in the Transvaal, he referred to his Kathiawar experience. That was a world of small towns. Here, he was dealing with urban India in Delhi or Bombay. The population was several multiples of the Indian population in the Transvaal, and had he known better, he would have anticipated the violence which resulted. Indian urban crowds are liable to be much more violent when aroused.

To begin with, a muddle occurred. He announced a hartal for 6 April 1919 several days in advance. But Delhi erupted a week earlier on 30 March. No one paid any heed to his appeal about refraining from violence, neither the rioters nor the police (obviously, the Indian bazaar had not caught up with MKG's political style). The hartal proper followed on 6 April. He was prevented from going to Punjab, which incensed more people. MKG said that he had made a 'Himalayan miscalculation'. He wrote to the viceroy: 'Rightly or wrongly, I seem to command, at the present moment, in an excessive degree, the respect and affection of the people all over India.'[29]

No one realized it, but the image of this frail-looking person, dressed down to look like the ordinary Indian, already called a Mahatma, and speaking in a totally different idiom from the better-known Congress leaders, had a larger mass impact than anything the Indians or the British had ever seen. Of course, unlike other Congress leaders, MKG had taken to incessantly

---

[29]Ibid., p. 81.

travelling around India, especially to small market towns and villages. His way of dressing and speaking in local languages appealed to people. No previous leader had been seen in small towns, let alone villages. Even so, the explosions were not over yet. Something much worse happened in the following week, and changed forever the attitudes of Indians towards the Empire.

On 13 April 1919, at a springtime festival (Baisakhi) in Amritsar, a crowd gathered to protest against some high-handed moves by the local administration. Amritsar had been tense for a week or longer, and there had been attacks on some White residents. There was a curfew. Then the local powers that be overreacted. General Dyer gathered soldiers at one end of an open space—the Jallianwala Bagh—and shot down the people who had no escape. Anywhere between 350 and 1,000 people died. Dyer was unrelenting. Indeed, he was feted by many who thought he had restored calm in Amritsar.[30]

The Jallianwala Bagh Massacre of 13 April 1919 has been etched in Indo-British history as the most unforgivable violent act committed by the British colonial government. It undermined the implicit faith many subjects of the Empire had in British justice and fairness. It transformed the status of MKG instantly. He challenged the Empire much more directly now. There was a lot of dry tinder lying around. He just had to put a match to it.

Surprisingly, at the London end, the government was much more critical of what Dyer had done. Montagu, being Jewish, was having a hard time defending the decision of the government to cashier Dyer. Churchill was sent into the Commons to take on the

---

[30]Desai, Kishwar, *Jallianwala Bagh, 1919: The Real Story*, HarperCollins, Delhi, 2019.

defenders of Dyer. He denounced Dyer's action as terrorist, and the massacre as 'a monstrous event' and not what one expected of British imperial rule.[31]

MKG in Charge

MKG argued for boycott of the elections on account of the Montagu-Chelmsford proposals for a dyarchy. He took charge of the Congress somewhat rapidly. Tilak died in 1920. By then, Gandhi had established his reputation as someone who could rouse a much wider section of Indians than the Congress had ever done before. Liberals such as C.R. Das from Bengal and Tej Bahadur Sapru did not like this style, and took a backseat. MAJ bided his time, and waited for MKG to fail, so the normal constitutional path could be resumed. He was not welcome at the Congress meeting as he would not call him 'Mahatma', but only 'Mr Gandhi'.

Then MKG chose an issue dear to the Muslims of India, and indeed, across the Sunni ummah. This was the future of the sultan of the Ottoman Empire, as well as his empire. The sultan was a Khalifa (Caliph), and the guardian of the holy places of Islam—Mecca, Medina and Jerusalem among them. The secret Sykes-Picot Agreement signed by the British Foreign Office and the French Quai d'Orsay, which divided up the Middle East between France and Britain, allocated Jerusalem to the British under a League of Nations trusteeship arrangement. The rumour was that the Caliphate would move to Jerusalem. This was not

---

[31] Desai, Meghnad, *The Rediscovery of India*, Penguin Random House, Gurgaon, India, pp. 136–39.

officially admitted in public. MKG became the champion of the Khilafat agitation which was initially led by Mohammad Ali and Shaukat Ali. The demand was to let the sultan remain the Caliph in Constantinople.

MKG had known Muslims in South Africa, but it is not clear if he knew much about the long history of the conflict between Islam and the West. The Crusades took place centuries ago, but the Christians of Europe had not forgotten that they had been defeated and driven out of Jerusalem by Saladin. Indeed, when the Portuguese arrived in India in the late fifteenth century, they waged a war against Muslims in South India.[32] The Ottoman Empire suffered a naval defeat in the Battle of Lepanto (1571) with the Habsburg Empire. The defeat of the Ottoman Empire in the First World War had been anticipated, which was why the secret Sykes-Picot Agreement was signed by France and Britain. They parcelled up the Ottoman territory between themselves for post-war control under League of Nations rules. This broader context was missed as MKG thought that the Khilafat movement would unite Hindus and Muslims in India.

It is not very likely that MKG was aware of the secret plans Britain and France had for the dismemberment of the Ottoman Empire. Not only did Britain and France conclude the secret Sykes-Picot Agreement which parcelled out the various territories of the Ottoman Empire between the two powers, Lawrence of Arabia was also freelancing in the Middle East, arousing the Arab chiefs of what are now Saudi Arabia, Qatar and the United Arab Emirates, by saying that the Allies would reward them with independence if

---

[32]See my book *The Rediscovery of India* on Alfonso Albuquerque waging war on Muslims, Chapter 2.

they helped in defeating the Ottoman Empire. There was also the Balfour Declaration made during the war, which promised help to Jewish groups to find a home in Palestine which the British knew they would administer after the war.

As far as the Allies were concerned, there was a new element which entered the arena during the war. This was the entry of the USA in the war on the Allies' side in 1916. Woodrow Wilson brought an un-European idealism to the war with his Fourteen Points. Lloyd George was driven by this as well as some domestic reasons of fighting the Pacifists, to declare in early 1918: 'The settlement of the new Europe must be on such grounds of reason and justice as will give some promise of stability... Government with the consent of the governed must be the basis of any territorial settlement in the War.' This was extended further. He promised 'genuine self-government to those Austro-Hungarian nationalities which desired it.' Extending these principles, he said the same principles should be applied outside Europe so that in case of the Ottoman Empire, the Turks would be left unmolested with Constantinople as their capital .... Arabia, Armenia, Mesopotamia, Syria and Palestine would be entitled to a recognition of their separate national identities.[33]

Of course, much of this, as applied to the Ottoman Empire, was only half-true, as Lloyd George was not revealing the real grabbing of the territories of the Ottoman Empire which was to follow the armistice. Many of these decisions were secret, and we know them now because of what happened. Woodrow Wilson was against the old European practice of grabbing the territories of defeated countries. Thus the prime minister was saying nice

---

[33]Rowland, Peter, *Lloyd George: A Biography*, Macmillan, New York, 1975, p. 428.

things in public, which he had no intention of abiding by. In any case, Lloyd George had to be sure that France did not come out of the war better off as far as the remnants of the Ottoman Empire were concerned. At least in this important instance, MKG's faith in British fair play was misplaced. This was the Perfidious Albion at play.

MKG opened up the Congress to ordinary membership at four *anna*s (one quarter of a rupee; four pence in the British currency then). Instead of a 'congress', i.e. an annual gathering of elite leaders, it became a political party with provincial offices, recruitment drives, and delegates elected to attend the annual conference. India was to have a mass political party. From his early days in London to his later visits from South Africa, MKG had seen the British Labour movement throw up a mass political party which was different from both the Liberal and the Conservative Parties—the Labour Party.

The weapon was non-cooperation. Participants were invited to give up jobs and honours they may have received from the British government, leave schools and colleges which had been started with government approval, and go to newly established national universities. The notion was that since India was ruled by a small number of British officers served by thousands of Indian officers, a strike by the Indian civil servants was bound to cripple the administration.

The response was overwhelming and India-wide. Muslims, who had only lately joined in the march for government jobs and college education made the bigger sacrifice. The older generation of Congress leaders refused to join in.

This was the first time in British Indian politics that a purely religious issue was being used as a cause for an anti-government campaign. It was also about an issue outside India, and with no implication for India's march towards self-government. MKG not only raised the theme of Hindu-Muslim unity to heights not previously seen, but also stretched the credulity of some of his followers. Indulal Yajnik, a young Gujarati who served as his secretary (and later went on to have a colourful literary career), expressed the puzzlement of these young followers:

> The question that then faced us was—if the Khilafat campaign could be construed even as a purely political fight under the banner of the Khilafat Committee (for we were then really called upon to fight under the banner of the Khilafat Committee under Mr. Gandhi's leadership as the issues of the Punjab and the political freedom had been left over for the consideration of the Congress that was to meet after a few months). In fine, what was our duty at this supreme moment? This was the question that began to be discussed in all political circles that were frankly perplexed and amazed at the increasing militant tones and tactics of Mr. Gandhi who began really to surpass even the most orthodox Mohammedans in his fanatical zeal for the cause of Islam.
>
> Now trying ourselves to rid India of the 'suzerainty' of the British Empire, we could not share Mr. Gandhi's enthusiasm for imposing the suzerainty of the Turkish Sultan over the outlying Provinces of Mesopotamia and Arabia. Perhaps we thought Mr. Gandhi had the excuse of his ignorance of Turkish history. Otherwise, he might have known better about the effects of the Turkish revolutionaries and about the ceaseless rebellion in which the Arabs of

Mesopotamia, Palestine and other provinces had broken out against oppression and barbarous misrule of the Turks in the past centuries.[34]

It is very much like a young, radical man to doubt the senior leader's knowledge of the outside world. Yajnik was not quite wrong. In his first big struggle in India, MKG wandered into unknown territory. The consequences were going to be long-lasting.

Lloyd George had a long-standing dislike of the Turks since when he was 13 years old (as we now know from biographies), and the news had come of Turkish atrocities in Bulgaria in 1876–77, which Gladstone had campaigned against. Lloyd George admired Gladstone. 'He was convinced that they [the Turks] were the ruffians of Europe—a band of cutthroats who ought to be exterminated—and that they had put themselves beyond the pale of civilised society.'[35]

MKG was not to know (though he may have had an inkling, it is hard to be sure) that the British policy was to encourage Greece to grab as much as it could of Ottoman territory at the end of the war. The faith MKG had in British imperialism was misplaced. Or at least, the radical Welsh prime minister—the first to come from outside the English aristocracy—was not going to play according to the rules. Lloyd George brought the country through a horrible war. The popular demand was for revenge and reprisal. He contested the November 1918 elections on the call 'Hang the Kaiser'. The Ottoman Empire was alien to Europe, and definitely to British sentiments. Indian Muslims may have placed

[34]Yajnik, quoted in Sayyid, Matlubul Hasan, *Jinnah: A Political Study*, Shaikh Muhammad, Kashmir Bazar, Lahore, 1945, p. 257.

[35]Rowland, Peter, *Lloyd George: A Biography*, Macmillan, New York, 1975, p. 564.

their faith in British power, but policy from the London end had no concern for Delhi's worries. There were rumours in the British press as to how much help Lloyd George had promised the Greeks.

In the middle of all this, in early 1922, Lord Reading, the new viceroy, sent a telegram to his secretary of state for India Montagu, which was critical of British policy on Turkey. Montagu released it to the press. No doubt, Reading was hinting at his own troubles. There was much trouble likely in Parliament because of this information being released by a cabinet minister and received from India via a Viceroy. Montagu had to resign. That saved Lloyd George's honour.[36] It should have been clear to all concerned, including English barristers, that the Khilafat movement would get nowhere. But MKG was looking only at India, not back at England.

MKG had uncharacteristically promised swaraj in one year. This was a very bold promise, even if the British Empire had been somewhat battered in the war. But like the Pied Piper, he charmed thousands to follow him. The British government was also dealing with several crises just at that time.

The war cost a lot in terms of men's lives and money. The Bank of England had gone off the gold standard (as it had during the Napoleonic wars). There was the outbreak of the Spanish flu which was a pandemic not seen in Europe for some centuries. There was inflation for the first time in a hundred years. Liberal Party was about to lose its power as the Conservative MPs were in no mood to continue with the coalition.

There was trouble in Ireland where the Sinn Fein won the argument over home rule for Ireland. There was a sectarian war

---

[36]Ibid., pp. 567–68.

between the Catholics and Protestants in Ireland, which was to lead to a partition, but that was still a few months away. The treaty with the Ottoman Empire was taking its time. Germany had been dealt a raw deal at the Versailles Conference, and was on the brink of hyperinflation. The Austro-Hungarian Empire had broken up into various linguistic 'nations'. Hungary, Poland and Czechoslovakia were formed—each jealous of its newly acquired independence. Indeed, the end of the First World War (as it came to be called later) saw an explosion of newly formed nations, and the beginning of unrest in the colonies of successful European empires.

Gandhi had given the viceroy a warning, but even so, he maintained communications with Lord Reading who had just taken up his position. Thus there was some doubt as to whether the Ali brothers were as committed to nonviolence as MKG intended. After meeting the viceroy in Simla during the summer of 1921, MKG was able to persuade the Ali brothers to issue a statement about their commitment to it.

The non-cooperation movement continued through 1921. There was violence in Bombay when the prince of Wales arrived on a visit. There had already been a Moplah rebellion in Kerala which took the form of Muslim workers in coconut activity rising against their Hindu landlords. This was a sign of danger in terms of communal warfare. But MKG seems to have been active travelling around India encouraging non-cooperation.

MKG had promised swaraj within a year, but the end of the year was approaching, as was a deadline of a week after 1 February 1922, given to the viceroy to release political prisoners who were already caught non-cooperating. The prediction of freeing India in one year loomed large. The new viceroy Lord

Reading was contemplating convening a Round Table Conference of Indian political parties. But then, on 4 February 1922, in the village of Chauri Chaura in the United Provinces, a crowd set fire to a police station in which many policemen lost their lives. Unilaterally, MKG suspended the campaign. This took everyone by surprise, and frustration was widespread. It was not as if there had not been sporadic instances of violence. It would have been surprising in a country of India's size if that had been the case. But to suspend a campaign while going strong, short of the promised date, when self-rule was going to be won, stunned everyone.

But MKG had his consultation with a Higher Authority. He explained:

> God has been abundantly kind to me. He has warned me the third time that there is not as yet in India the truthful and non-violent atmosphere which and which alone can justify mass disobedience. He warned me in 1919 when the Rowlatt Act agitation was started. Ahmedabad, Viramgam, and Kheda erred, Amritsar and Kasur erred. I retraced my steps, called it a Himalayan miscalculation, humbled myself before God, and man. The next time it was through the events of Bombay God gave me a terrible warning. He made me eye-witness of the deeds of the Bombay mob on 17th November. It was not my intention to stop the Mass Civil Disobedience which was to be immediately started in Bardoli. But the bitterest humiliation was still to come. Madras did give me warning but I heeded it not. But God spoke clearly through Chauri Chaura.[37]

---

[37] Sayyid, Matlubul Hasan, *Jinnah: A Political Study*, Shaikh Muhammad, Lahore, 1945, pp. 284–85.

In short, he confessed that he had repeatedly misjudged the capacity of the Indian mob to be disciplined and nonviolent. In South Africa, he only conducted limited disobedience campaigns, and his followers were indentured labourers or merchants familiar with the violence the police could unleash. In his ashram, he could order his friends to follow his commands about cleanliness and sex. This time though, not only was the scale massively bigger, but also the actors were way beyond his control.

He was the sole arbiter of what was and was not the issue. Thus, his challenge to the viceroy to release the political prisoners or face civil disobedience now had to be abandoned. But then, there were sacrifices required:

> But Chauri Chaura has raised another immediate issue, namely, terrible penance of a fierce process of purification, and this penitential purification requires sacrifice of the imprisoned workers and the temporary sacrifice of many of our activities which have revived the nation. But such things happen in all wars, much more frequently than in spiritual warfare as ours is claimed to be. When I heard of Chauri Chaura I sacrificed them as the first penitential Act. They have gone to jail to be released only by the strength of the people; indeed, the hope was the Swaraj Parliament's first act would be to open the prison gates. The prisoners can now only gain by serving the full term of their imprisonment.[38]

In writing to the viceroy, he did, somewhat subtly, blame the Muslims. As he put it: 'I confess that I did not—I did not attempt it—succeed in weaning them (the Party of violence, that is the

---

[38]Ibid., p. 285.

Muslims under the Ali brothers) from violence on moral grounds, but purely on utilitarian grounds.'[39]

Even so, his command was not challenged. Anyone else confessing how often he got things wrong (despite God's warnings) would have faced a massive rejection. Many explanations have been given why MKG did what he did. Of course, he did not take anyone into his confidence. He was the sole leader as he always preferred to be. People were perplexed, angry, frustrated, but obedient. Somehow, his charisma was overwhelming, and perhaps this sheer, surprising irrationality was his effective weapon. Jawaharlal Nehru, who had just come under his influence, and was tasting the hardships of political agitation, tried to rationalize why MKG could have done what he did:

> Gandhiji has often acted almost by instinct; by long and close association with the masses he appears to have developed as great popular leaders often do, a new sense which tells him how the mass feels, what it does and what it can do. He reacts to this instinctive feeling and fashions his action accordingly and later for the benefit of surprised and resentful colleagues tries to clothe his decision with reasons. This covering is often inadequate, as it seemed after Chauri Chaura.[40]

This is a young, rational, Cambridge Natural Science Tripos graduate struggling to find a defence for someone who had won him over. Nehru's impatience with MKG was to last much of their life together, and yet he never wavered from his admiration, not

---

[39]Desai, Meghnad, *The Rediscovery of India*, Penguin Random House, Gurgaon, India, p. 145.
[40]Ibid., pp. 285–86.

to say his devotion, for Gandhi. MKG remained, and remains, an inexplicable phenomenon as a mass political leader.

Gandhi's Hinduism

There was an obvious difficulty with Gandhi's approach which has not been pointed out as far as I am aware. (What follows is my own interpretation of Gandhi's ideas.) He developed his own version of Hinduism away from daily life in India. Hinduism is not a single monolithic religion like the Abrahamic faiths. There is no single book which is authoritative, nor a priesthood which interprets the single Truth. His religion, which derived much from his mother and father, was a form of Gujarati Vaishnavism, but was influenced by Jainism (especially through his discussions with Raychandbhai). Add to that his familiarity with Christianity, especially the nondenominational church of Methodism. Gandhi avoided temples and worshipping any icons. His prayer meetings consisted of simple singing of hymns. This is very much how Methodists worship, without any incense, or partaking of wine or wafers, as the Church of England or the Catholic Church do. He also studied Esoteric Christianity. This sect believed that it was Jesus Christ and his life that were the essence of Christianity. Christ took on all the sins of mankind to rescue it. Gandhi personalized this idea inasmuch as for the rest of his life after leaving England he blamed himself, as for example, when his Indian followers, or just ordinary people, did not behave as he urged them or expected them to behave. The most dramatic example of this was when much later, in the mid-1940s, he blamed himself over the violence in the Noakhali riots, attributing them to his failure to adhere to brahmacharya. In the middle of the riots, he tested his resolve on brahmacharya with the help of his great-niece Manu Gandhi and shared his agony with the readers of his newspapers. He was in his mid-seventies by then. It scandalized his best friends and followers. His Hinduism was his own private construction. It became a problem when he began to lead the masses in India. And display it in public.

Ahimsa, which formed the core of Gandhi's philosophy of satyagraha, is more to do with Jain or Buddhist beliefs than Hindu ones. The *Shakta* stream of Hinduism as it is practised in regions like Bengal would not tend towards ahimsa. Indeed, the Bhagavad Gita, Gandhi's favourite text, starts with Krishna telling Arjuna, the hero of the Mahabharata, why it is right for him to kill his cousins, or indeed, his *dharma* as a Kshatriya to battle against his enemy relatives. Ahimsa was incorporated into Hinduism after the advent of Buddhism and Jainism. Had he spent his early adult years in India, there would be no reason for him to expect the bazaar on a hartal to be nonviolent. Educated, middle-class civil servants or university students might have been cognizant, but nothing in Indian history says that Hindus are nonviolent. Not when there is a designated caste, Kshatriya, whose dharma it is to kill. Savarkar, whom he had already met in London, did not share Gandhi's view of Hinduism, nor did the Arya Samaj which was popular in Punjab. Hence, Maharashtra, Punjab and Bengal would neither understand nor follow Gandhi's Hinduism.

After Khilafat

The anti-climax came when Mustafa Kemal Pasha, the new ruler of Turkey, abolished the Khilafat, and established a secular state in Turkey. Palestine, which included Jerusalem, became a British mandate territory, and as the Balfour Declaration said, it was going to be receiving Zionist refugees. MKG did not seem to have been aware of this larger context. Indulal Yajnik, his young secretary who was also a socialist in those days, knew better when he pointed to Gandhi's ignorance about the Ottoman Empire. In supporting the Khilafat movement, Gandhi bit into something he could not chew. Indeed, it was something he should have not ventured into at all.

The one positive lesson MKG drew from this experience was that he never again launched a mass civil disobedience campaign. The way post-Independence India's historians, especially Congress favourites, have shaped the story of the fight for Independence, it is Gandhi's 1922 noncooperation, Gandhi's 1930 Salt Satyagraha, and Gandhi's 1942 Quit India Movement which delivered freedom. Such a simplistic reconstruction of history has done a lot of damage. But it is clear that for the Salt Satyagraha, Gandhi chose his 70–80 fellow marchers carefully. It was not a mass movement, though others did copy his act of salt-making. Quit India had to do without Gandhi and the Congress leadership because they were all locked up before the morning it was supposed to start. What followed was a violent attempt by young Indians—Jay Prakash Narayan and Aruna Asaf Ali emerged as leaders—in the 1942 campaign to disrupt India's attempt to defend the Empire at home and abroad. It was not nonviolent. It was put down severely.[41]

MAJ had seen this coming. He was not charmed by MKG. He remained a Liberal Constitutionalist. He had no liking for

---

[41]Desai, Meghnad, *The Rediscovery of India*, Penguin Random House, Gurgaon, India, 2009, pp. 232–40.

religion being brought into politics (ironic though that may sound to the present generation). His response to Gandhi's invitation to him to join the movement was forthright. He wrote to MKG:

I thank you for your kind suggestion offering me 'to take my share in the new life that has opened up before the country'. If by 'new life' you mean your methods and your programme I am afraid I cannot accept them; for I am fully convinced that it must lead to disaster. But the actual new life that has opened up before the country is that we are faced with a Government that lays no heed to the grievances, feelings and sentiments of the people; that our countrymen are divided; the Moderate Party is still going wrong; that your methods have already caused split and division in almost every institution that you have approached hitherto and in the public life of the country not only amongst the Hindus and Hindus and Muslims and Muslims and even between fathers and sons; people generally are desperate all over the country and your extreme programme has for the moment struck the imagination mostly of the inexperienced youth and the ignorant and the illiterate. All this means complete disorganisation and chaos. What the consequence of this may be, I shudder to contemplate; but I, for one, am convinced that the present policy of the Government is the primary cause of it all and unless that cause is removed, the effect must continue. I have no role or power to remove the cause; but at the same time I do not wish my countrymen to be dragged to the brink of a precipice to be shattered. The only way for the Nationalists is to unite and work for a programme which is universally acceptable for the early attainment of complete responsible government. Such a programme cannot be dictated by any single individual, but must have the approval and support of all the prominent Nationalist leaders in the country and to achieve this end I am sure my colleagues and myself shall continue to work.[42]

This rather long reply is a hint of the coming parting of the ways. MAJ stayed on his Liberal Constitutionalist path. There was no separate mention of Muslim interests, not even his passionate pursuit of a proper, proportionate share for the minority. This was a national leader of long standing telling a newcomer of a few years' standing that his own path would not change from what it had always been, not even for the promised new life. It was more or less a parting of the ways, though the style of the letter was not unfriendly despite being in deep disagreement. Indeed, as we shall see later, the two continued on the same broad path, though with different methods, for a few more years.

But MAJ was no less angry with the British about their treatment of Turkey. As he said then:

> ...notwithstanding the unanimous opinion of the Mussalmans and the breach of the Prime Minister's solemn pledges, unchivalrous and outrageous terms have been imposed upon Turkey, and the Ottoman Empire has served for plunder and broken up by the Allies under the guise of Mandates. This, thank God, has at last convinced us, one and all, that we can no longer abide our trust either in the

---

[42]Wolpert, Stanley, *Jinnah of Pakistan*, Oxford University Press, New York, 1984, p. 70.

Government of India or in the Government of HM the King of England to represent India in matters international.[43]

Jinnah was obviously more clear-headed about the motives of the British than Gandhi was. MKG decided that after Chauri Chaura he would devote himself to his constructive programme. He had to serve his prison sentence, of course, but the days of hectic activity were to cease for a while. MAJ, on the other hand, was still at work, never having renounced the idea of competing in the elections. So he stood for the Central Legislature again, but as an independent candidate. His statement said:

I have purposely not put forward the grounds of my claim to your support, as I feel that my part in the political life in our country since 1906 when I first attended the annual session of the Indian National Congress has been before the public; and ever since, I have endeavoured to the best of my abilities and judgment to serve the cause of the people. Of one thing, I can assure you, that the popular cause and welfare of India will be my keynote and the guiding principle in the future, as, I hope, it has been in the past.[44]

He further reinforced his credentials in those turbulent days in a speech to the Muslim League at its Lahore session in 1923:

While that demand [for swaraj] is a just one and the sentiment only natural and requires all encouragement, we must not forget that one essential requisite condition to

---

[43]Sayyid, Matlubul Hasan, *Jinnah: A Political Study*, Shaikh Muhammad, Lahore, 1945, p. 258.
[44]Ibid., p. 308.

achieve Swaraj is the political unity between Hindus and Muslims; advent of foreign rule and its continuance in India is primarily due to the fact that the people of India, particularly the Hindus and Muslims are not united and do not sufficiently trust each other... Swaraj is almost an interchangeable term with unity.[45]

Here was MAJ staying true to his life's mission as a nationalist Liberal Constitutionalist who held on to the message of Hindu-Muslim unity. But in a way, the context was changed by MKG. The days of constitutional action were over. MKG had upset the apple cart, and although he set it or tried to set it the right way up, the consequences of what he had done altered the context in which MAJ thought he could still operate. But then, MKG was never straightforward to interpret.

Despite the surprising aspect of MKG's sudden cancellation, it is a question worth asking why he did it. In a way, MKG had issued a warning and a deadline to the viceroy. This direct communication with the top was one element of his style which was new to Indians. He had, of course, gone straight to the top in South Africa, though without much success. He always parlayed one to one with the top interlocutor on the other side. He would not enter Parliament's portals, and move resolutions. That was not his style. He had asked the viceroy to release all those who had already begun non-cooperation, and were arrested within a short period after the start of the movement. Poor viceroy! He stood no chance of complying since the movement was suspended as Chauri Chaura happened on

---

[45]Ibid., pp. 309–10.

5 February. Rufus Isaacs (Lord Reading), the viceroy, had not been in India for a long time. Back home, the situation was getting worse, the coalition government was in trouble. Ireland was about to be lost.

One straightforward explanation is that until Chauri Chaura the violence had been among the people themselves, and was of the communal-riot variety. But in Chauri Chaura, it was the police representatives of the state who were the victims. They were killed while performing their duty. It could just be that MKG took the view that such an effect of his call to the people was difficult to defend. Of course, he did not explain this.

It could just have been (and this is my conjecture) that MKG saw the trouble brewing back in Britain, and wanted to save His Majesty's Government any embarrassment. (After all, Montagu was forced to resign as a side effect of Turkish developments.) He behaved like His Majesty's 'Loyal Opposition'. He let the government off the hook. My evidence is speculative. But after Chauri Chaura and until the start of the Second World War when the Congress refused to behave like a loyal opposition, Gandhi could always directly reach out to the top as he did with Lord Irwin in 1930 when he became the first common subject to parley with the viceroy on terms of equality. It was not till another war and Lord Linlithgow becoming the viceroy that MKG launched non-cooperation, one way or another. MAJ turned the tables, and became the loyal opposition, and won his place at the viceroy's side. But I am running ahead of our story.

The events following Chauri Chaura were deeply disturbing. The split between Hindus and Muslims opened up wide. The Hindu Mahasabha was formed 10 years earlier, but coexisted with the Congress with leaders like Pandit Madan Mohan Malaviya active in the Congress as well. But now, the riots spread between Muslims and Hindus on the usual issues of cow slaughter and music outside mosques across the Indo-Gangetic plains where there was a close habitation of both communities. Agra and Delhi saw Hindu-Muslim riots. Swami Shraddhanand, a prominent Hindu Mahasabha politician, was murdered.

The calculus of minority and majority proportions of Hindus and Muslims, which had been valorized by the Montagu-Chelmsford Reforms, led to a movement among Hindus to reconvert Muslims, whose ancestors may have changed from being Hindu to being Muslim (as indeed MAJ's family had), back to Hinduism. This was called the *shuddhi* (purification) campaign. The Lucknow compromise worked by MAJ seemed ages ago. As things stood, there developed a split between those who wanted to boycott the elections to the provincial assemblies following MKG, and the Swaraj Party of C.R. Das, Motilal Nehru and other senior leaders who wanted to fight the elections. The aftermath of Chauri Chaura helped the Hindu Mahasabha get many more of its candidates elected. MKG might have thought that he was launching a combined Hindu-Muslim movement to get swaraj within a year, but the effect of his initiative and its suspension was exactly the opposite. Most Muslim politicians moved away from the Congress. Those few who remained—elite Ashrafi Muslims—were labelled nationalist Muslims by the Congress. The Muslim League recruited many more *ulema* now than had joined them before.

When the aftermath of Chauri Chaura was working its consequences on Congress politics, MAJ was still sticking to his constitutional route. He had never been in favour of boycotting the elections to the legislatures as MKG advocated. The Swaraj Party, which had made a (friendly) break with the Congress, won seats in the Assembly, but so did the Hindu Mahasabha. MAJ's platform of Hindu-Muslim unity was under threat. But he was not ready to give up.

He was still in the Central Legislative Assembly along with the Swaraj Party. He was happy to form a nationalist coalition with them. So he moved a resolution on constitutional reform in the Assembly in February 1924. The resolution recommended an 'early' summoning of a Round Table Conference to discuss, among other matters, 'the protection of the rights and interests of important minorities,' and 'to take steps to have the Government of India Act revised with a view to establish full responsible Government in India.' The resolution was carried 76 to 48, and Lord Reading, the viceroy, appointed a Reforms Inquiry Committee. Jinnah became a member of the committees, along with Sir Tej Bahadur Sapru, a leading Liberal, and the mathematician R.P. Paranjape (known as Wrangler Paranjape since he got a first class in his Mathematics Tripos at Cambridge). It became known as the Jinnah Committee.[46] When the report came out, given its strong tone, the viceroy vetoed any discussion of its recommendations.

Undaunted, MAJ then got an agreement by passing a resolution in the Assembly to ask the government of India to tender for its purchases in India as well as in London so that some of the public expenditure of India would stimulate Indian business. This was the case during the Great War, so it could be resumed.

---

[46]Wolpert, Stanley, *Jinnah of Pakistan*, Oxford University Press, New York, 1984, pp. 80–81.

Dadabhai Naoroji raised this issue in his classic indictment of British-rule poverty and 'Un-British rule' in India. MAJ was, after all, a long-time follower of Dadabhai.

In May 1924, MAJ presided over a special session of the Muslim League in Lahore. This was his comeback, as it were, after being rejected by the Congress (for not calling MKG 'Mahatma'). He was back to his normal themes centred on Hindu-Muslim unity. As he said:

> Boycott of Councils as desired by Mahatma Gandhi, was far from being effective or useful... the Khilafat organisation, which was carried on, could not claim any better position... The result of the struggle of last three years has this to our credit that there is an open movement of *Swaraj* for India. There is a fearless and persistent demand that steps must be taken for the immediate establishment of Dominion Responsible Government in India.

He added: 'One essential requisite condition to achieve *Swaraj* is political unity between the Hindus and the Mohammedans... I am almost inclined to say that India will get Dominion Responsible Government the day the Hindus and Mohammedans are United. *Swaraj* is an almost interchangeable term with Hindu-Muslim unity.'[47]

Further, 'viewing with great alarm the deplorable bitterness of feeling at present existing between the Hindus and Musalmans, the League further resolved to cooperate in establishing "conciliatory boards" on which members of all communities could meet

---

[47]Wolpert, Stanley, *Jinnah of Pakistan*, Oxford University Press, New York, 1984, pp. 82–83.

regularly to resolve communal differences, and try to alleviate causes of conflict.'[48]

But the time for resolutions in well-organized meetings was fast disappearing. The genie was out of the bottle. Religion had been harnessed as a rousing principle. It could not be used as a uniting one. Whatever one might say, and whoever one may blame, the Khilafat agitation as well as its failure to deliver swaraj within one year as promised, and then its suspension, marked a dividing line between old methods which MAJ championed, and the new direct action that MKG pioneered. When self-government did come, Hindus-Muslim unity was the first casualty.

On the eve of his departure, Lord Reading did offer MAJ a knighthood, but Jinnah declined: 'I prefer to be plain Mr. Jinnah. I have lived as plain Mr. Jinnah and I hope to die as plain Mr. Jinnah.'[49] Jinnah was sincerely an Indian, though an anglicized one, thanks to his stay in London. But he knew that titles like 'Sir' offered by Reading were not worth their signal that the possessor had sold his soul for a mess of pottage.

But Jinnah was ready to serve on the Sandhurst Committee appointed by the Assembly to inquire into the feasibility of establishing a military college in India. He visited England, as a result, taking his wife along, visiting military colleges and installations overseas, spending the summer months between April and August in Europe. It combined work which was his main concern all his life, sparing some time with his wife who was slowly sinking.

Ten years later, Dr Ansari, a prominent Muslim member of the Congress, put before MKG a tabular comparison of the difference

---

[48]Ibid.
[49]Ibid.

in the state of Hindu-Muslim unity before and after Khilafat.[50] He showed how in 1920, there was the 'highest water mark reached in Hindu- Muslim unity.' By 1930, it was the 'lowest mark reached in Hindu-Muslim unity.' In 1920, there was 'complete unity inside the Congress.' In 1930, there was 'disunity in the Congress, diversity of purpose, complete lack of enthusiasm amongst the workers.' After Chauri Chaura, all talk of Hindu-Muslim unity became partial wish-fulfilment on the part of the Congress. The upper-class Ashrafi Muslims from UP stayed with the Congress, while poorer, ordinary Muslims floated away.

A crucial development in this period was the realization of the obvious geographical fact that there was a bunching of the few Muslim-majority provinces in two far corners of British India. One was the cluster in the northwest with Punjab, the North-West Frontier (not yet called a province), and Balochistan, though that was a 'princely state' and not a part of British India. Then an obvious extension of this 'Muslim corner' of British India was seen to be on its edge as Sind, which was part of the large Bombay province. If Sind could be made a province on 'administrative grounds', rather than communitarian ones, it would create a corner with four Muslim-majority provinces. As and when self-government came into operation, these neighbouring Muslim-majority provinces would form a useful cluster. At the eastern end, Muslims knew from the experience of the Bengal Partition that they had a slight majority in Bengal, perhaps with Assam in addition to it. Muslims lost out when the Partition of Bengal of 1905 was reversed in 1911. They would have another

---

[50]Guha, Ramachandra, *Gandhi: The Years that Changed the World: 1914–1918*, Penguin Random House, Gurgaon, 2018, p. 327.

chance with the Montagu-Chelmsford Reforms.

On the Hindu Mahasabha side, the Khilafat campaign had brought about the realization that India was at the eastern end of a cluster of Muslim nations stretching to Turkey and Egypt. Lala Lajpat Rai was articulating his worry about these Muslim nations combining forces to support their brethren in India. These ideas seem like a fantasy nowadays, but the First World War had disturbed the serenity of the men who thought the British Empire would protect them from all outside forces. Now MKG had himself seen the geographical shadow Islam cast on India. He had obviously come to conclusions which meant that the Muslims of British India could be helped by their Hindu brethren to remove the British, as they would be helped by their neighbouring Muslim brethren to fight for the Caliphate. The logic proved faulty for India, but its inverse became part of a belief in India that Muslims could unite across borders to invade Hindus.

Were Muslims a Minority or a Nation?

It is difficult now to imagine how large and powerful the Ottoman Empire was, and what a pivotal role it had in European history. While its capital city Istanbul or Constantinople symbolized the point of convergence of Europe and Asia, the empire did occupy what now is Southeastern Europe. Yugoslavia, as it used to be, plus Rumania, Bulgaria and parts of Southeastern Russia belonged to the sultan. The Muslims had run across North Africa and captured Spain in the first millennium of the Common Era. All that we now think of as the Arab Middle East was in the Ottoman

Empire. This empire had a continuity with what had begun in the eighth century with the advent of Islam.

In effect, Sunni Islam had its empire—not individual nations or kingdoms. Indeed, the idea of a Sunni Muslim 'nation' was heretical. Through much of history, territory was divided into kingdoms or empires. Subjects of the monarch or the emperor were loyal to the person of the king or the emperor, who in case of Sunni Muslims was the Khalifa. It was only when the empires broke up and became republics like the American colonies of England or France in 1789 that a new consciousness of a people or a nation arose. Then the loyalty was to the abstract entity—the nation. The question then arose as to who was part of the nation and who was an alien. Mohan and Muhammad had no difficulty going to England, studying or working there. No visas were needed. They were subjects of the Empire. They were welcome despite the fact that they were not English.

The end of the First World War brought a particular sort of crisis to Islamic consciousness. While the Austro-Hungarian Empire could break up and generate 'new' nations—Hungary, Poland and Austria—the idea of single Muslim nations was controversial. Iqbal, a poet and a philosopher, had been thinking about the crisis caused by the end of the Ottoman Empire. Iqbal was educated in Lahore and then Europe, before coming back to Lahore. He wrote a long poem 'Shikwa' (Complaint) which was his complaint to God about the sorry state of Islam. Later, he also wrote a 'Jawab-e-Shikwa'.[51]

Iqbal, like MAJ, was influenced by British education (Trinity College Cambridge, same as Jawaharlal Nehru), but also had been

---

[51]'The Reply to Complaint', See Desai, *Rethinking Islamism*, 2007.

to Germany. He was not restricted merely to the Indian context by having to think of minority rights or majority opportunities. Nationalism was, after all, a European notion introduced by the French after the Revolution of 1789. France ceased to be a Bourbon kingdom, and became a nation of citizens. It already had a territory and a long history, a language, and it was predominantly a Catholic Christian country. It launched a movement to liberate neighbouring kingdoms and their people, and unleash modernity. Much of European history since 1789 has been wars waged by France against other European kingdoms, especially the Austro-Hungarian Empire and the German principalities, especially Prussia. Napoleon's invasion of what is now Germany sparked the birth of nationalism in that land. Along the way, the idea of a nation was developed in the German kingdoms. Here, they went into their hoary past. The claim was that Germans were an ancient nation with an old language. Its territory was split up into various principalities of unequal sizes. Even in terms of religion, the Reformation created divisions, which led to the Thirty Years' War (1618–48). But the Germans came up with a story about how and why they have been a nation for centuries.

There is no single definition as to what constitutes a nation. Indeed, much of the century since the end of the First World War saw numerous upheavals within and between territories on the question of nationhood. To begin with, no nationalist agrees that the idea of nationhood is a modern, i.e. nineteenth century, idea. Each nation believes that it is ancient, if not timeless; the Older, the more legitimate. Forces such as a common religion, language, race (which in itself is a tricky concept), and contiguous territory are all meant to define a nation.

The lives of MKG and MAJ together were devoted to sorting out (however unsuccessfully) the ambiguities of whether India was one nation or two, whether each nation within India had a single contiguous territory. A majoritarian view held by the Congress, especially nationalists such as Nehru and Maulana Azad, was that India was a single nation as a result of the joint common history of the people over centuries. India was neither a Hindu nor a Muslim nation exclusively but accommodated the two religious communities. This was the prevalent view of what is known as the Awadhi syncretic culture in UP, which had the largest population among all Indian provinces, but also the largest Muslim population, albeit as a minority. Awadhi culture, also known as *lakhnavi tehzeeb*, became Nehru's idea of a secular India. The elite Muslim populations of UP stuck with the Congress. The other Muslim view held by MAJ was that as self-government came nearer, the minority status of Muslims numerically meant that their interests had to be protected against the danger of a Hindu majority dominating the Muslim minority. Once voting—rather than royal decrees—decided the issues, the majority and minority, if permanent, could split the nation. The Liberal counter-argument is that religion is not the sole determinant of the interests of an individual or a group. Jawaharlal Nehru considered religion to be unimportant, if not dangerous, in defining national identity, and believed that cross-religious alliances—secular behaviour—are possible and healthy for the nation. MAJ was not religious. He was, as I have mentioned before, a Liberal Constitutionalist; but he was concerned about the rights of Muslims as a minority.

But even the minority-majority question was not one which

had an unambiguous answer in the Muslim context in India. It depended on what kind of political structure a self-governing India was going to have. To begin with, in the late 1890s or the early 1900s, the question was the composition of the Imperial (Central) Legislative Council. This was a small-size body, and the elected element was a part of it. Here, separate electorates did not matter, and the minority proportion was agreed upon in Lucknow, in 1916, with the Congress working out the proportion in each province.

The Montagu-Chelmsford Reforms took the focus to provincial legislatures. Here, the crucial fact emerged that in some provinces Muslims had a majority, but in most provinces they were a minority. Some states where they had minority rights were still provinces with large populations, such as UP. So a small percentage still yielded a large number of seats. Thus the calculus of majority and minority kept changing in a kaleidoscopic way.

The issue that awaited was what sort of powers would be given to the provinces as against the Centre. Montagu-Chelmsford had opened up the issue of allocation of provincial ministries along popularly elected legislators as against official ones. But the Congress was wedded to the idea of a strong Centre, since it expected to be in power as a majority community party. The Muslims preferred what Americans call a 'States Rights' approach. Maximum permissible autonomy for the provinces meant that Muslim-majority provinces could be (almost) self-governing vis-à-vis the majoritarian Hindu Centre.

India was debating these issues while it was still legally a part of the British Empire. Indeed, a view often denounced as heretical was that there was no single territory called India with its current boundaries till the British established sole control over it by 1857. The idea of India itself was an outcome of a foreign conquest. This maddened the nationalists, especially the orthodox Hindu Mahasabha nationalists. For them, the idea of India as a nation was not modern but ancient, if not eternal. It was Muslims who were alien intruders in their view, and did not belong to the authentic *ur*-India, the *rashtra*.[52]

Thus, Indians were fighting to throw off foreign rule, while still defining what it was that they were liberating. Being an articulate and argumentative people, well-read in several languages and knowing many traditions, there was no shortage of disputes. Add to that British Constitutional norms and rules (which, after all, were going to determine the shape of the outcome), and what you would get would be a feast for those who had 'been called to the Bar', as several of the leadership had been.

The question which became crucial as the end came nearer (though, again, without hindsight, no one could tell in advance) was whether there were two nations as well as two separate nation-states in India.

The breakthrough that Muhammad Iqbal arrived at was the discovery that in the northwest corner of British India, adjacent to Afghanistan with which the Durand Line had been marked out

---

[52]This was also why the theory of an 'Aryan invasion' of India during remote pre-Christian era was deeply disliked by Hindu nationalists. An 'Aryan invasion' meant they were outsiders who had come in unwelcome. Hindu traditionalists wanted to be able to put the label of alien invaders on Muslims who came after the advent of Islam in the eighth century of the Common Era. If there were autochthonous Indians who had inhabited India before the advent of the Aryans, Hindu traditionalists did not want to know about them. This is one reason why dates in prehistory of India are highly speculative.

as a boundary, was a cluster of four Muslim-majority provinces which combined the idea of a nation as a collectivity with a homogenous religious persona and a contiguous territory—a nation, in principle and as a territory. This idea was to later overwhelm the constitutional debate about minority rights which had been ongoing, by presenting a new alternative.

However, once again, we must avoid hindsight. In 1930 when Iqbal spoke to a pathetically small gathering of 30-odd delegates of the Muslim League, no one was thinking of two sovereign nation-states. Even when the word 'Pakistan' was thought of, there was no idea of an independent India as an achievement happening in the lifetime of the various leaders. What was going on was speculation about the constitution of the next stage of the limited self-government under the watchful eye of the British Parliament. The Congress, which was by now thinking of itself as the sole organization representing all Indians, wanted a federation with a strong Centre, more or less on the lines of the British arrangement they were living under. Jinnah was worried about the protection of minority rights if the foreign ruler was to be gone. The Muslim idea was that they had to extract some sort of promise from the British that whatever self-government scheme was to be brought in, it would give due weight to minority rights.

Hence, the preferred option for Jinnah and Iqbal was a federation with a weak Centre, but lots of autonomy at the provincial level. If that could be conceded, then a group of four Muslim-majority provinces could be brought together to provide extra clout to the Muslims. No one got so far as envisaging the British gone, or even one, let alone two, nation-state being created.

The principal difficulty with this idea was that the Muslim

population of these four states was a small proportion of the total population of Muslims in British India. Even when Bengal and Assam at the opposite end were added as two more Muslim-majority states, the anomaly remained, namely that a majority of Indian Muslims lived in Muslim-minority states while the Muslim-majority states comprised a minority of the Muslim population. The Muslim nation was geographically split whichever way you cut the cake.

MAJ saw that the issues of large and small as versus majority and minority mattered less than the number of Muslim legislators there would be at the Centre. That was the shape of the government on offer. Hence, he persuaded the League to drop its insistence on separate electorates, but accept joint electorates. There were other demands added, such as the separation of Sind from the Bombay province, and making it a province on its own with the Montagu Chelmsford Legislature, along with regularizing the status of the North-West Frontier District as a province. MAJ was ready to be flexible once he could operate on a national canvas.

FOUR

THE FAULT IN OUR STARS

H ence, there was a premium to preserve the 'Union' (a word used in the US about the federation, especially at the time of the Civil War) on the part of the Muslim leadership. All the contracting parties—the British government, the government of India, the Congress and the Muslim League— wanted a settlement. The destination was known, but not the timetable. The abrupt end of the Khilafat agitation in 1922 led to MKG taking his 'sabbatical', dropping out of active agitation, and spending his time on constructive work—cotton-spinning, rural uplift, and basic education, which were very dear to him, and to which he could harness the energy of others. It was important to him, and he argued that these activities would bring freedom closer, but it was irrelevant, passive time-pass for the rest of the independence movement.

His Majesty's Government was not idle, however. The failure of non-cooperation convinced them that they could stick to their timetable. MKG (as per my interpretation) was not going to come in their way in any major disruptive fashion. He remained a loyalist. So they moved to the next stage in the Government of India Act, 1919, i.e. Montagu-Chelmsford Reforms, which had promised that Parliament would review its working after 10 years. Lord Birkenhead, secretary of state for India, jumped the gun to appoint such a commission while the Tories were still in power lest the Labour

Party, likely to give India away for a song, came to power next. So the appointment of the Simon Commission was announced. By parliamentary rules, the act specified that only MPs and lords could review the working of the act. But the Congress objected to the absence of anyone from India. The new viceroy Lord Irwin (Edward Wood, MP, who was the eldest son of Lord Halifax, had his peerage 'accelerated' while his father was still alive to be made viceroy of India) did suggest that Indian members be included. But Birkenhead was not as favourably inclined towards India as Irwin. The Simon Commission was to receive a report from the Central Legislative Chamber, but that was not enough for the Congress. So it boycotted the commission. The League was split. One wing welcomed the commission. Jinnah's group rejected it.

Jinnah said:

A constitutional war has been declared on Great Britain. Negotiations for a settlement are not to come from our side. Let the Government sue for peace... Lord Birkenhead has declared our unfitness for Self-Government. I welcome Pandit Malaviya and I welcome the hand of fellowship extended to us by Hindu leaders from the platform of the Congress and the Hindu Mahasabha... This is indeed a bright day; and for achieving this unity, thanks are due to Lord Birkenhead.[53]

His thanks to the noble lord was precipitate. Hindu-Muslim unity did not flourish.

---

[53]Guha, Ramachandra, *Gandhi: The Years that Changed the World: 1914-1918*, Penguin Random House, Gurgaon, 2018, pp. 90–91.

This boycott looms large in Congress history, but it failed to stop the commission from visiting and meeting Indians in various regions, and producing a comprehensive report. Attlee was a member of the Simon Commission—though a reluctant one, as he was afraid it would take him away from British politics, and elections were coming again soon. But his going turned out to be significant as it shaped his ideas about how to tackle Indian self-government.[54]

The answer to the Indian complaint that they were not given a chance to join the exercise Simon was to carry out was a rude one—that Indians would never agree among themselves even if they tried, but conveyed in more polite terms. Stung by that, the various parties got together into an All Party Conference mode, and appointed a large committee under the chairmanship of Motilal Nehru. The Motilal Nehru Committee laboured well and produced what became an early draft of independent India's Constitution. A universal franchise was there, as was a strong Centre. It did not accept Jinnah's revised stance regarding joint electorates, Sind, or anything else. By then, the Hindu Mahasabha's M.R. Jayakar had become very influential. The Mahasabha was not keen on any concession for the Muslims. MAJ was very disappointed. His campaign over the preceding 20 years had now come to a roadblock. After this, any joint action on Hindu-Muslim unity or a shared vision was impossible. The end of the 1920s devalued that saga. It had begun with MAJ being a leading Indian nationalist politician. The Congress had been a reformist annual gathering of the Hindu and Muslim elite. Now it was a mass political party

[54]Desai, Meghnad, *The Rediscovery of India*, Penguin Random House, Gurgaon, India, 2009, pp. 149–70.

run by MKG. There was nothing for MAJ to do. As it happened, he lost his young wife Ruttie in February 1929, leaving behind a 10 years old daughter. He left India as London would be a better home for him.

The Round Table: An Opportunity Missed

Much of the history of this period available in India is obviously from an Indian (even post-Partition Indian) perspective. It revolves around the Congress and its policies. But the active principle now was His Majesty's Government (HMG). There had been a hiatus in governments in Whitehall between 1922 and 1924. The war-time Liberal-Conservative coalition broke up, and was replaced by a Conservative prime minister (Bonar Law), and after his early death, Stanley Baldwin, as the new leader, called an election. To everyone's surprise, the recently born Labour Party came to power for the first time (the king was worried if the incoming Labour Cabinet would know how to dress up for meeting him as his Privy Council!). By 1924, the Conservatives were back in power with Stanley Baldwin at the helm, and Churchill as chancellor of the exchequer. (Churchill had left the Liberal Party, and just migrated to, but not as yet made himself unpopular in, the Conservative Party, and had not relegated himself to the back benches as he did five years later.) Baldwin became prime minister in preference to Curzon because there was a democratizing upsurge in Britain. Lloyd George was the first commoner (with no aristocratic connections, unlike Asquith) to become prime minister. His rise was due to a split in Asquith's Liberal Cabinet during the war. Lloyd George was also the first Welshman to become prime minister. Now it was an Englishman's turn. Baldwin sat in the House of Commons. By this time, all adult men above 21 years of age and all women above 30 had the vote. Commons was the dominant Chamber of Parliament. The king emperor took the view that henceforth prime ministers would be sourced from the House of Commons and not the House of Lords. By 1928, women had full franchise, same as men.

From here on till 1947, the pace of constitutional reforms was unrelenting. It was Whitehall pushing, not Congress prodding. Of course, whatever was offered was rejected by the Congress as not enough, not purna swaraj. But it was as if the British had a game plan. The Morley-Minto Reforms in 1909 were followed by the Montagu-Chelmsford Government of India Act, 1919. The Simon Commission came in 10 years later. Parliamentary committees in London discussed the Simon report, and groups of lords and MPs visited India to look at the situation till the Government of India Act, 1935, was enacted. It was a hectic situation, though again, the Congress was complaining as was its habit.

There began then an unprecedented consultation of diverse interest groups of Indians at the Round Table Conference in November 1930. The first session lasted from 12 November 1930 till 19 January 1931. The Labour Party was again in power. The next two sessions were from 7 September 1931 to 1 December 1931, and the third and last one met from 17 November 1932 to 24 December 1932. The first conference was in the middle of the Great Depression, and the Labour government was worried as to what it could do about rising levels of unemployment. During the second conference, MacDonald's government went through a crisis, and a National (coalition) Government was asked to take office by the king. This was the biggest crisis in modern British history. By the time of the last conference, the Labour Party was split and a coalition government with Conservative dominance, retaining MacDonald as prime minister, had come in. However, Stanley Baldwin, leader of the Conservative Party, was not as against Indian self-government as Churchill and the die-hards of the Conservative Party were.

But that was later. At the first two sessions, Ramsay MacDonald was active as the host and the prime minister. He had travelled to India before the First World War, and written his impressions in a book, *India Awakening*. He had also served as a member of the Islington Commission in 1912, which was to advise on the Indianization of the civil services in India. Jinnah had met him, along with Gokhale, in London, then in their capacity as members of the Imperial Legislative Council. There is some evidence that it was MAJ who took the initiative of writing to Ramsay MacDonald, whom he had known since 1912, and met since his return to London. He suggested a wide consultation of Indians, which would bring in representatives beyond the parties behind the Motilal Nehru Report. MacDonald sent a friendly reply, saying he was about to do what MAJ was advocating.[55] The idea was to consult the various 'interests' in India as to what the next step for constitutional change would be after Simon. This would be a concrete response to the Indian complaint that they were not consulted. But again, the British idea of who should be consulted was much broader than that of the Congress (though not MAJ),

[55]Wolpert, Stanley, *Jinnah of Pakistan*, Oxford University Press, New York, 1984, p. 109.

which thought it was the sole body worth consulting. The Congress refused to join in the first session held in November 1930. MAJ was there not as a Muslim leader—he represented himself as he had been a member of the central legislative body for nearly 20 years. The Aga Khan was there to represent the Muslim League.

Again, since the Congress did not participate in the first Round Table, Congress historians in independent India have dismissed it as a failure. The conference was, in fact, a major effort by a Labour prime minister sympathetic to Indian aspirations to bring together many Indians, including representatives of the princely states, trade unionists, women, representatives of minorities— Muslims, Sikhs, Christians, as well as untouchables (represented in all three sessions by Dr Ambedkar). The Congress missed out on this massive discussion on the shape of the future Constitution of India. Its stance was that the Motilal Nehru Report was the answer. By now, Hindu Mahasabha leaders, especially M.R. Jayakar, were influential on the national stage, and Hindu-Muslim unity was not their platform. Hence, the Motilal Nehru Report was Hindu majoritarian inasmuch as it rejected Jinnah's proposals for joint electorates.

There were three parties present at the Round Table Conference as the British saw it—the British government, British India and Indian India, namely the princely states. Early on in the conference, the maharaja of Bikaner (who had been in the Indian delegation to the Versailles Conference in 1919) declared that in any future self-governing India, the princely states would like to join. This was a massive step to unite all of India under self-government. India was going to be a federation. The principal questions debated by the conference over its three sessions were the details of the Centre, its powers as well as the degree of autonomy for the provinces, the size and powers of the legislative chambers, franchise details, reservations for minorities—women and Christians, among others. Financial arrangements were discussed as to the responsibilities and resources of the Centre and the provinces. It was a major exercise in preparing early drafts of the future Constitution of a self-governing India. The 1935 act was the legislative outcome of this process. Had the Congress taken a whole-hearted participative role, it could have shaped the 1935 act better. But that is a conjecture on my part.

The conference was inaugurated by George V in the Royal Gallery of the House of Lords (the most sumptuously decorated room, with paintings and illuminated windows). The throne, which is normally within the chamber of the House of Lords, was moved a few yards across to where the inauguration of the Conference was to be. It was said to be the only time the king emperor sat at the same level as his subjects! But they all stood while the emperor spoke. There were delegates from the British government (16), the princely states (16), and from British India (57). MacDonald was proposed as chairman of the conference, and unanimously voted in. Speeches from the delegates followed. Among them was Jinnah's speech following that of the Liberal leader Srinivas Sastri, who was a veteran of the Indian political scene as a member of the Viceroy's Assembly for many years. Jinnah stuck to his tough demands:

> I am glad Mr. President (MacDonald) that you referred to the fact that the declarations made by British sovereigns and statesmen from time to time that Great Britain's work in India was to prepare her for self-Government have

been plain. But I must emphasize that India now expects translation and fulfilment of these declarations into action.[56]

In the absence of the Congress, Jinnah was the most important leader the British had to deal with. In a sense, he was rewarded for two decades of membership of the Viceroy's Council where he had taken a nationalist line without fail.

After the inauguration, the conference moved to St. James's Palace. Prime Minister Ramsay MacDonald played an active part in it. In the absence of the Congress, the Hindu Mahasabha was well represented by M.R. Jayakar and Dr Moonjee. Their stance on the Muslim question was pretty much clear; they were hostile to granting any concessions to the minority. Jinnah came to the first two sessions.

The absence of the Congress at the first session did not prevent the delegates from taking up the question of minorities. As MacDonald presiding over the session recorded in his diary for 14 December 1930: 'Yesterday a Moslem-Hindu gathering at Chequers [the weekend residence of the prime minister] showed worst side of Indian politics... India was not considered. It was communalism & proportions of reserved seats.'

By 18 December, he was even gloomier: 'Hindu-Moslem not coming together,' he noted. 'They have no mutual confidence & Hindu too nimble for Mosl. brethren. Hindu can appear to be reasonable because he has the pull.' The Moslem leader Jinnah, he added, assured him that the conference must fail.[57]

---

[56]Wolpert, Stanley, *Jinnah of Pakistan*, Oxford University Press, New York, 1984, p. 119.
[57]Marquand, David, *Ramsay MacDonald: A Political Biography*, MacMillan, 1977.

On 13 January, he noted, 'Busy day with interviews, most important being Mohammedans headed by Aga Khan with Shafi and Jinnah… Practically threatened civil war if their claims for Security were not admitted. They would not trust Hindus, nor cooperate with them on terms of confidence. They begged me to settle now—in their favour of course.' It was not just Hindus and Muslims as was thought until now. He continued, 'The Sikhs were equally intransigent.' 'Great tussle at St. James' Palace over Hindu-Moslem question,' MacDonald noted on 14 January. 'Brought it to verge of settlement in Punjab, but Sikhs stood out against the pressure of every section—on 1. Opposition to 50% of the Seats going to Moslems. 2. Refusal to accept any proposition under 20% for themselves.'[58]

Almost 90 years later, we should appreciate MacDonald's awareness of the Sikh dimension which was ignored in 1947, at the time of the Partition, but has lingered up to now in the form of the claim for Khalistan. There were not just two sides in the communal question. Since the Congress was not there, the Hindu side's representation fell to the Hindu Mahasabha. In a way, this indicates why the Congress's idea that it was the sole representative of India was overblown and inaccurate. A great opportunity was missed due to such hegemonic arrogance.

The main obstacle of the Hindu-Muslim question was not settled despite two more sessions, the second of which MKG attended as the sole Congress delegate. Again, negotiating in a conference with other delegates was not his style of settling an issue. He would have preferred, no doubt, a one-on-one meeting with Ramsay MacDonald, just as he did with the viceroys. But

[58]Ibid.

here he had to cope with other delegates such as the Aga Khan as well as Muhammad Iqbal who also came only for the second session. Jinnah was a part of the Minorities Subcommittee of the second session, but there is no record of whether he participated. He might have left it to Iqbal to look after Muslim interests.

The Congress having sent Gandhi as its sole delegate (Mahadev Desai went as a secretary and Sarojini Naidu was the women's representative), the conference could be excused for thinking as Guha put it:

> By coming to London as the sole representative of the Congress, Gandhi was offering to the British people the syllogism INDIVIDUAL=PARTY=NATION. Gandhi was the Congress which was India. This presentation was flatly rejected by the other Indian participants at the Round Table Conference. And it was denied by British Government too.[59]

But even Gandhi himself was reluctant to accept this 'syllogism'. As Guha said:

> As Mahadev (Desai) wrote to Nehru, their mutual master 'had two most disappointing interviews with Shaukat Ali and the Aga Khan'. While Jinnah was better 'he wondered why Gandhi was adamant that any agreement on Muslims had to have the approval of Dr. Ansari'.[60]

It turns out that in earlier discussions in the Congress as to who would go to the Round Table Conference, Gandhi had

---

[59]Guha, Ramachandra, *Gandhi: The Years that Changed the World: 1914-1918*, Penguin Random House, Gurgaon, 2018, p. 407.
[60]Ibid., p. 406.

received advice from Charles Andrews, his friend and an old India hand, that:

> ...he bring Madan Mohan Malaviya, Jawaharlal Nehru and M.A. Ansari to make the delegation more effective. Others thought he should take Sarojini Naidu, whose charm and speaking skills would help win over the British public, which had lately come around to the view that women could vote and become MPs too. However, Gandhi was insistent that he alone would represent the Congress.[61]

Here, again, was Gandhi's early South Africa model of being the sole leader or spokesman if he took up a cause. But as we can see from Mahadev Desai's letter, he either regretted that judgement when he arrived in London, or just invoked Dr Ansari as the extra person needed, who alone could back up his (Gandhi's) judgement to whether or not accept concessions demanded by the Muslims (i.e. Jinnah) at the conference.

So 'syllogism' or not, Gandhi was not going to settle the Hindu-Muslim question in London. As he was undoubtedly a truthful person par excellence, it would be useful to conjecture about what happened to change his mind. After all, if he had thought Dr Ansari was necessary for Hindu-Muslim negotiations, he could have taken him along as he did Mahadev or Meera, his British daughter. Guha, in his chapter on this episode, says:

> At the Karachi Congress, in March, Gandhi had been nominated the party's sole representative at the conference.

---

[61]Ibid., p. 388.

Even while he was in India, however, Gandhi began having second thoughts about this. To now ask for more representatives would be to lose face, and also perhaps to play favourites—if the government agreed, who among Nehru, Patel, Rajagooalachari, Kripalani and Rajendra Prasad would he take along, and who would he leave behind? Instead, he asked both Willingdon and Irwin to nominate Dr. M.A. Ansari as a delegate from the Nationalist Muslim Party. They declined, the Viceroy writing that 'I'm afraid I can do nothing about Dr. Ansari but if the S(ecretary) of S(tate) chooses to nominate him of course I should raise no objection.'

Shortly after reaching London, Gandhi told a representative of the *Bombay Chronicle* that 'whoever committed the blunder of preventing Dr. Ansari from being selected as a delegate was responsible for committing a blunder.' In truth, he had contributed to the blunder himself. For Dr. Ansari was Member of the Congress. Once that organisation had decided to have only Gandhi as its representative, it was hard for Ansari to be invited.[62]

This was strange, not to say a serious mistake. To begin with, the Congress wanted to be the sole invitee to the Round Table on the grounds that India was Congress, and Congress was India.

That was a pretence the British Government could not take seriously. But having made that mistake, when the Congress changed its mind and got on the train for the second session, why choose just Gandhi? Was it because it was his style of leadership—to be the sole leader—since South Africa? Even so, if Mahadev and Mira

---

[62]Ibid., p. 399.

could go with him, and if he had decided that any concessions made by Congress for Muslims would have to be approved by Dr Ansari, why did he not take Ansari along as a useful companion (not a delegate, just as Mahadev was not one), in any case?

It might be (again, conjecturally) that he realized only after coming to London that there was a formidable contingent of Muslim delegates with Iqbal and Zafrullah Khan, as well as Shaukat Ali, Fazl-ul-Haq and Jinnah. This is why when it came to his turn on the Minorities Committee, he played 'a straight bat'. In the style of Indian batsmen of his time, he just blocked every delivery and stayed not-out, but scored no runs! Let me elaborate.

Firstly, on the British side, the country was facing the biggest political crisis ever. The Labour Cabinet was split on the economic policy required during the Great Depression. The Bank of England was not sure if they could defend the value of the pound. MacDonald knew that his Cabinet as well as his parliamentary party was divided. He wanted to resign. But the king emperor requested him to stay, and put together a national government with the support of the Conservative and Liberal parties. He accepted the challenge. MacDonald was forevermore reviled as a traitor by the Labour Party. All this happened during the last week of August 1931, just before the second session of the Round Table Conference.

The second report of the Minorities Committee signed by Ramsay MacDonald (18 November 1931) revealed:

At the first meeting of the resumed [i.e. since the first RTC] Committee on 28 September, it was reported that informal negotiations were proceeding between certain of the communities concerned, and after discussion, it was unanimously agreed that, in order to give these negotiations an opportunity to reach a conclusion, the Committee should adjourn until 1st October. On its meeting on that day, a further motion of adjournment until Thursday 8th October, to enable continuance of negotiations, was moved by Mr. Gandhi and unanimously accepted. It was agreed that the problem of the Depressed Classes and other smaller minorities would form part of the communal problem which was to be the subject matter of the conversations.[63]

Obviously, the conference was looking to MKG to solve the communal issue. That, after all, was what he had come for. But as the report continued, 'At the third meeting of the Committee on Thursday, 8th October, Mr. Gandhi reported that the negotiations which had taken place had unfortunately proved abortive, despite the utmost anxiety on the part of all concerned to reach a satisfactory outcome.'

What Gandhi did was to present the Congress policy on the minorities question by citing the Motilal Nehru Report on a take-it-or-leave-it basis. (The document from which I am quoting is the official summary of the proceedings of the three sessions of the RTC. It appears as Appendix I in the *Report of the Committee on Minorities*. The three separate reports, one for each of the sessions, were bound together.[64])

[63]His Majesty's Stationery Office, *Indian Round Table Conference (SECOND SESSION) 7th September, 1931—1st December, 1931, PROCEEDINGS*, January 1932, https://tinyurl.com/59mxuba6. Accessed on 10 April 2024.
[64]This publication was made available to me by the House of Lords library. Ibid, pp. 62–63.

The Congress scheme for a communal settlement (circulated at the request of Mr M.K. Gandhi) was: [65]

However much it may have failed in the realization, the Congress has, from its very inception, set up pure nationalism as its ideal. It has endeavoured to break down communal barriers. The following Lahore Resolution was the culminating point in its advance towards nationalism.

In view of the lapse of the Nehru Report,[66] it is unnecessary to declare the policy of the Congress regarding communal questions, the Congress believing that in an independent India communal questions can only be solved on strictly national lines. But as the Sikhs in particular, and the Muslims and other minorities in general, have expressed dissatisfaction over the solution of the communal question proposed in the Nehru Report, this Congress assured the Sikhs, the Muslims and other minorities that no solution thereof to any future Constitution will be acceptable to the Congress that does not give full satisfaction to the parties concerned.

So in this document laid before the RTC, the Congress is precluded from setting forth any communal solution of

[65]I have cited a document prepared for me by the House of Lords library in the proceedings of the Round Table Conference in my text. These passages are from the documents quoted in that report.

[66]'The lapse of the Nehru Report' refers to the notice the Congress had unilaterally given to the government of India that if the Motilal Nehru Report was not accepted within its offer of a time frame of one month, noncooperation would be resumed. The GOI ignored this warning; hence, the Lahore pledge of purna swaraj taken by Jawaharlal Nehru as president of the Congress in December 1929.

the communal problem. But at this critical juncture in the history of the Nation, it is felt that the Working Committee should suggest for adoption by the country a solution though communal in appearance, yet as nearly National as possible and generally acceptable to the communities concerned. The Working Committee, therefore, after full and free discussion, unanimously passed the following scheme:

1 (a) The article in the constitution relating to Fundamental Rights shall include a guarantee to the communities concerned of the protection of their cultures, languages, scripts, education, profession and practice of religion and religious endowments.

   (b) Personal laws shall be protected by specific provisions to be embodied in the constitution.

   (c) Protection of Political and other rights of minority communities in the various Provinces shall be the concern and be within the jurisdiction of the Federal Government.

2. The franchise shall be extended to all adult men and women.

(Note A: The Working Committee is committed to adult franchise by the Karachi resolution of the Congress and cannot entertain any alternative franchise. In view, however, of the misapprehension in some quarters, the Committee wishes to make clear that in any event the franchise shall be uniform and so extensive as to reflect in the electoral the proportion in the population of every community.)

3. (a) Joint electorates shall form the basis of representation in the future Constitution of India.

[Note B: Wherever possible, the electoral circles shall be determined as to enable every community, if it so desires, to secure its proportionate share in the legislature.][67]

4. Appointments shall be made by non-party Public Service Commissions which shall prescribe the minimum qualifications, and which shall have due regard to the efficiency of the Public Service as well as to the principle of equal opportunity to all communities for a fair share in the Public Services of the country.

5. In the formation of Federal and Provincial Cabinets interests of minority should be recognised by convention.

6. The N.W.F. Province and Baluchistan shall have the same form of government and administration as other Provinces.

7. Sind shall be constituted into a separate Province, provided that the people of Sind are prepared to bear the financial burden of the separated Province.

8. The future Constitution of the country shall be Federal. The residuary powers shall vest in the federation Units, unless on further examination it is found to be against the best interest of India.

The Working Committee has adopted the foregoing scheme as a compromise between the proposals based on undiluted communalism and undiluted nationalism. Whilst on the one hand, the Working Committee hopes that the whole Nation will endorse the scheme, on the other, it assures those who take extreme views and cannot adopt it, that the Committee

---

[67]Note B is not part of the scheme but has been added by me as not being inconsistent with the scheme. (Introduction) M.K.G.

will gladly, as it is bound by the Lahore resolution, accept without reservation any other scheme if it commands the acceptance of all the parties concerned.

October 28th, 1931

The point of listing this document presented to the Minorities Committee is to give more details on what MKG did at the Round Table Conference where he was, by assumption, the plenipotentiary representative of the Congress. But the way the Lahore Resolution was presented and the proviso 'Hence, the Congress is precluded from setting forth any communal solution of the communal problem' was to say that while he was there, he would not or could not enter into any negotiations on this vital issue with other interested parties. Did he come determined not to concede anything on the vital Hindu-Muslim question?

If he was not there to consult and bargain with the other parties—the British government and Muslim and Sikh representatives—why was he there? The document I have quoted from also lists several more views held by the other parties on this vital, not to say the biggest, issue he had come to settle. Dr Moonjee attached a memorandum on the Congress formula, suggesting amendments. In Appendix III, there was also 'Provisions for a settlement of the Communal Problem Put Forward jointly by Muslims, Depressed classes, Indian Christians, Anglo-Indians and Europeans'. Appendix IV was titled 'Sikhs and the Constitution for India'. There was a memorandum by Sir Chimanlal Setalvad. There were also memoranda in women's interests including one by Sarojini Naidu. There were 20 separate appendices listing the memoranda submitted by the delegates on the questions of minorities defined broadly as women and workers, as well as Muslims, Sikhs and Indian Christians.

The historical accounts of the conference and what MKG did hardly mention these other memoranda, or even the presence of other Indian delegates. Indeed, there is in his biographies more about his extracurricular activities in East London and Lancashire than the job he was sent to do.

The tone of the Congress resolution put before the Minorities Subcommittee by MKG seemed to say 'take it or leave it'. This could mean either that his freedom to bargain was limited or non-existent, or that not bargaining was his own decision, which hardly seems likely.

(It is a side issue but there is some evidence that MKG met Ramsay MacDonald one on one. My evidence for that is that the statue in Parliament Square was modelled on a photograph of MKG coming out of the doors of 10 Downing Street. There was no mention of such a meeting in the biography of MacDonald from which I have already quoted. This is a puzzle I have been unable to solve.)

At the Karachi Congress, there were mutterings about his failure to get a pardon for Bhagat Singh. The Congress also adopted a radical socialist economic programme which went against MKG's preferences, thanks to the emergence of Nehru, Subhas and other young Congress members. Did he notice that a new generation was ready to take over? So did he take this tough stance knowing he had no real plenipotentiary powers? The majoritarian stance of the younger generation was winning over. Jawaharlal had no sympathy for religion as a basis for nationalism.

Anyway, the Congress had overestimated its strength or

Gandhi's likely impact. Other invitees had come to do business, for all knew that this Round Table was not a trivial event. In the midst of the worst economic crisis, London already had a conference inviting the White Commonwealth nations to debate the thorny issue of tariffs and Imperial Preference just days before holding the Round Table on India. It seems that neither the Congress nor Gandhi wanted to bargain. The Motilal Nehru Report was the only and final offer.

The Minorities Subcommittee, at this time, had 57 members, the British government had 11 including the prime minister, and the rest were from British India as the representatives of the princely states did not think they had to contribute to this issue. Twelve of the Indian representatives were Muslim, including the Aga Khan, Maulana Shaukat Ali, Maulavi Shaji Daudi, Sir Muhammad Iqbal, Sir Sultan Ahmad, Sir Muhammad Shafi, Dr Shafa'at Ahmad Khan, Begum Shah Nawaz (Bhutto), Zafrullah Khan and Fazl-ul-Haq. Jinnah, of course, was also there, but not as a Muslim representative; he was there as a member of the Imperial Legislative Council.

The Hindu representatives were G.D. Birla, M.K. Gandhi, Sir Padamji, Dr N.M. Joshi, Pandit M.M. Malaviya, Sir Provash Chunder Mitter, Dr B.S. Moonjee, Sarojini Naidu, Diwan Bahadur A.T. Pannir Selvam, Diwan Bahadur Ramachandra Rao, B. Shiva Rao, Mr Srinivas Shastri, Sir Chimanlal Setalvad, Rao Bahadur Srinivasan and Mrs Subbarayan.

Of course, Dr Ambedkar was there as well, but I doubt if he would have counted himself as a Hindu.

(I have given these mundane names to indicate the extent and width of representation at the RTC. Since the Congress was not an active participant, except for this one session with one representative, an impression is conveyed by Indian biographers and historians of this period that the RTC was just Gandhi being there briefly and no one else. This was far from being the case.) At the end of the first session (when the Congress was absent), the Minorities Committee concluded in its report:

> ...(I)n order to ensure that the cooperation of all communities which is essential to the successful working of responsible Government in India, it was necessary that the new constitution should contain provisions designed to assure the communities that their interests would not be prejudiced, and that it was particularly desirable that some agreement should be come to between the major communities in order to facilitate the consideration of the whole question.

Resuming the deliberations in its second session starting on 28 September, and subsequently 1 October, 8 October and 13 November, the committee noted that 'It had the assistance in the discussion of the representative of the Congress Party.'

Gandhi did not push seriously for any result, and came back to India. What he did achieve was a greater face recognition among the ordinary British public—be it in the East End of London or in the Lancashire textile mills. He had an audience with the king emperor, and even met Charlie Chaplin.

From the first session onwards, MacDonald had signalled the crucial importance of settling the communal issue. At the conclusion of the first session, he said:

> Everyone must honestly admit that situations have arisen, like some of the communal difficulties, which have put

obstacles in our way. Now, I want you to take it from me
that the attitude of the British Government in such relations
is nothing more than an overpowering desire to leave you
to settle your own affairs. We are not pro-Hindu, we are
not pro anything else. If we are animated by anything, it
is by the conception of India herself—India feeling behind
and below and above and beyond her communal differences
that mystic bond of unity which the us Great poets, the
great philosophers, the great religious teachers of India have
always felt. Believe me, the British Government has no desire
to use your disagreements for any ulterior purpose. Quite
the opposite. Our one ambition is that, being in a sense
kith and kindred with you, (since history whether you like
it or whether we liked it, has woven our destinies somehow
together.), we may use that unity with you in order to pave
your way and smooth your path to that much-required
internal unity amongst yourselves.[68]

The British economy, once the leader in the world, had suffered
much in the First World War. The Bank of England went off the
gold standard for the duration of the war, and did not return to
it until 1925. When he was chancellor of the exchequer, Churchill
submitted to orthodox financial advisers, and returned the UK
to the gold standard at the old parity. Keynes famously wrote
a pamphlet 'The Economic Consequences of Mr. Churchill
criticizing that decision as likely to deepen the recession already

---

[68]'Prime Minister's Remarks at the final plenary session 19/1/31',
His Majesty's Stationery Office, *Indian Round Table Conference (SECOND
SESSION) 7th September, 1931—1st December, 1931, PROCEEDINGS,* January
1932, https://tinyurl.com/59mxuba6. Accessed on 10 April 2024.

there in the economy'. The weakness of the British economy was perhaps one cause for the return of the Labour Party to power in 1929, but by 1931, it was clear that the city and the international financial markets were doubting British economic strength.

As it happened, when he went to submit his resignation to George V, the king advised MacDonald to stay on as prime minister and form a National (coalition) Government. MacDonald was surprised, but agreed. This split the Labour Party, which henceforth described him as a traitor. By the time the Round Table Conference gathered again, the National Government was in office with MacDonald as prime minister, but with a Conservative majority and hardly any Labour members joining MacDonald.

Thus the session that MKG chose to attend was already under a cloud, as the Labour Party which was sympathetic to India was out, and the Conservatives were in. Even so, the pace of the Round Table Conferences did not slacken. No doubt the Conservatives had a different view, but extreme anti-India MPs like Churchill were out of favour, and relegated to the backbenches. The leader of the Conservatives, Stanley Baldwin, kept up the pace of the discussions about constitutional developments in India even after MacDonald departed.

But in the second session, it was the communal issue which was the highlight. Muhammad Iqbal was there as a 'new member', as was Gandhi. The conference set up various subcommittees at the first session. Jinnah, for example, was on the important subcommittee on the Federal Constitution where, one presumes, his participation secured the status of a province for Sind and the North-West Frontier. For the second session, he was on the

Minorities Commission where Gandhi was also present. But we have no note of Jinnah's activity.

As prime minister, Macdonald did propose a separate electorate for the untouchables after the conferences ended. But MKG, who was, by then, in Yerawada Jail, went on a fast unto death on the grounds that the untouchables were part of Hindu society. Dr Ambedkar, who had won that concession after much hard work, was furious. But he could not fight MKG who was threatening to die. He had to sign the Poona Pact (Yerawada was near Poona [now Pune]). While MKG himself did not sign the pact, Congress representatives did on behalf of Hindus, and Ambedkar on behalf of the untouchables.

What this showed was that whatever his public pronouncements, MKG was astute in anticipating what was coming. He could figure out before anyone else that the elections for the federal legislature would be proposed with separate electorates for Hindus and Muslims. His anxiety was the reverse of the one experienced by MAJ; he wanted to guard the majority position of Hindus, and not let it be diluted by the untouchable votes being hived away, whatever he may have thought about the evils of untouchability. Politics was all about securing a majority and hanging on to it.

In many subsequent exchanges, while MAJ accused the Congress of being a representative of Hindus, which Nehru and MKG denied, Jinnah never pointed to the Poona Pact which the Congress had signed on behalf of Hindus. He went on criticizing the Hindu attitude towards untouchables, but did not see how MKG had garnered a political prize from that anomaly.

The First Instalment of a Constitution for India

The Government of India Act, 1935, was a massive piece of legislation—the longest debated by the British Parliament till 1999 when it was surpassed by the Government of London Act. In framing it, the most elaborate parliamentary procedure was followed. The Simon Commission's report was studied by a joint committee of both Houses of the Parliament. Then followed various subcommittees of MPs, and delegations visiting India to meet local leaders. Then a draft bill was prepared by the government. The British economy was going through a crisis of Depression and had to abandon the gold standard. The Labour government, as we saw above, fell to be replaced by a National Government headed by MacDonald, with a large Conservative presence, and a small number of Labour MPs. But through it all, a massive draft bill was presented to the Parliament.

Being a constitutional bill, all its various stages including the second reading, the committee stage, the report, and third reading had to be taken on the floor of the House of Commons. (The House of Lords follows this procedure for all its bills. In the Commons, bills at the committee stage are discussed by a Select Committee of the House with members chosen by the leaders of each party.)

The bill had many novel aspects. The problem of native states was discussed with a view to including them in a self-governing India. India was to be a federation with a large degree of autonomy for the provinces. Self-government was to be confined to the provincial level. At the Centre, the governor-general or viceroy would rule with a Central Legislature which would be advisory. There was a list of subjects—some exclusively in the domain of the provinces, some in the domain of the Centre, and some concurrent. Elaborate rules were drawn up for revenue-sharing between the Centre and the provinces. This was a serious blueprint of the last but one stage of the journey to self-government. There would be elections with separate electorates.

The action had to now shift to the ballot box. MKG had been trying to revive civil disobedience on one or the other ground, but, by and large, getting nowhere. As a viceroy, Lord Irwin had been indulgent to him, though conceding little. Willingdon, who succeeded him, had previously been the governor of Bombay, and suffered the severe displeasure of MAJ during his time there. But he was an old India hand, and thus was unyielding. MKG was getting frustrated. The advent of the 1935 Act meant that elections were in the offing. The younger leadership of the Congress wanted to compete in the elections, and not boycott it as they had tried with Montagu-Chelmsford, split, and let the Mahasabha in. MKG then resigned from the Congress.

This was a shrewd move on his part. He could see that the principle of self-government had been granted, though details had to be worked out. MKG was never a details person. He had no desire to hold office. What was more, he was getting on. In 1934 when he resigned (it would be more appropriate to say that he dropped out) from (the day-to-day running of) the Congress, he was 65 years old. He had been subjecting his physique to experiments of diets and even more fasting, which must have been taking its toll on his health. He had to have an operation for his appendix, about which the ever-critical Churchill noted that he had resorted to Western medical practice after all.

My conjecture is that he was getting beyond constant hard

work after all these years. The events since Chauri Chaura had showed that his judgement could be not just surprising but also ineffective. Irwin definitely ran rings round him, and younger Congress members noticed that he could not get a reprieve for the martyr Bhagat Singh. Young socialists like Nehru and Subhas Bose were impatient to move away from God and towards Lenin. The Karachi Congress had passed a radical economic package which caused a split between the Right represented by figures such as Sardar Patel and Rajendra Prasad, and the Left represented by figures such as Nehru and Subhas Bose.

Gandhi was losing his grip and his interest. He made an infuriating statement that the Bihar earthquake was God's punishment for the practice of untouchability by Indians. Nehru, sitting in a prison elsewhere, was outraged by this outdated superstitious nonsense. Rabindranath Tagore was furious. MKG was getting more eccentric as the Congress Party leaders could see. But they also knew that he was the single most effective symbol keeping the mass party together. So while they let him drop out, everyone knew that he would be there when they pulled the emergency cord.

There was also a major change in MKG's perspective about the younger generation. This is my conjecture, but it bears examination. Motilal Nehru had pushed his son forward for Congress presidency in 1929. Indeed, Jawaharlal was to succeed his father immediately as Congress president. After some hesitation (as Patel was his senior, and should have succeeded Motilal), MKG agreed. Then Motilal died soon afterwards. Jawaharlal turned to Gandhi as his surrogate father. For Gandhi, this was the eldest son he never had—almost the same age as Harilal, but much better behaved.

So MKG acquired a surrogate son, and Jawaharlal a second father. The succession had now been secured.

He was still their great teacher, but the policy of the party was to be run by Jawaharlal Nehru, Sardar Patel and the younger lot. What Gandhi bequeathed to them was a mass political party which could be harnessed to fight elections. The Mahatma stuck to constructive work. He had vowed never to return to his Sabarmati Ashram in Ahmedabad if he did not deliver swaraj after the Salt Satyagraha. So he moved to Wardha where a new ashram community was assembled.

MAJ had a problem. Although he had taken up residence in London, he kept on sailing back to India. He had not given up his membership of the Central Assembly. So when the 1935 Act was announced with elections in the offing, who else to lead the Muslims but MAJ! But he did not have a fighting mass party nationwide. The Muslim League was more like how Congress used to be in the pre-MKG or pre-Khilafat days—an elite gathering.

Now the old Liberal Constitutionalist MAJ had to follow the MKG way; not only was it something that he did not like, it was also without a populist style using religion as a war cry. Jinnah had to be Gandhi without God in his armoury. It was going to be a difficult act to emulate. Of course, MKG was out of active operation. Elections and ministries were never a concern for him. He had secured a Hindu majority by forcing Ambedkar to give up separate electorates. He had cemented the majority.

What triggered the crisis for MAJ was the result of the 1937 elections caused by the 1935 Act. Provinces now had autonomy of a sort, but the Centre was still run by the governor-general. Each province had separate electorates, but the franchise was restricted according to the ownership of property. The Congress contested in Hindu as well as Muslim constituencies, while the Muslim League stuck to Muslim seats. The results were a shock for MAJ.

There were 1,585 seats in all; 808 were general (Hindu) and 482 were Muslim. Scheduled caste seats, part of the Ambedkar-Gandhi Pact, were 151. There were 41 seats for women, and 24 for tribal and backward areas. Nehru, as the de facto leader, with Patel as the organization man, was the new face of the Congress. As a radical socialist, Nehru played with the idea of boycotting the act, and then changing his mind, contested it, but promising to hopefully destroy it from within. MKG knew that once elected, the Congress would love power.

Congress won 711 out of 1,585 seats; excluding the Muslim seats, 683 out of 1,103 or 62 per cent of the seats. It had majority in five states, plus Bombay where it could form a government. All the provinces Congress won, except for the NWFP, were in what became India after Independence. Winning the NWFP thanks to Khan Abdul Ghaffar Khan gave Congress a Muslim cover. The Muslim League, on the other hand, won only 100 seats out of the 472 Muslim Seats. In Punjab, it was the Unionist Party led by Sir Sikandar Hayat, which confirmed its majority. The League won only 7 out of 84 seats in Punjab.

MAJ suffered a shock to his expectations. The League was still like the pre-Gandhi Congress, a talking shop, not a mass political party. In UP, a Muslim-minority state but a populous one, the League had hoped that the Congress would include its representatives in the government. UP had what the Congress boasted was the syncretic culture of Hindu-Muslim coexistence. But having got a majority, the Congress was in no mood to be nice to the Muslim League. This, after all, was normal British practice after an election. The party winning a majority formed the government. There was no need for a Congress-Muslim League coalition. The Congress had enough Muslims of its own in UP.

Khaliquzzaman was leader of the UP Muslim League, but had belonged to the Congress previously. He was hopeful of a coalition, but there was no scope for one. The Congress had a majoritarian view, and also believed that it represented Muslims just as well as the League did.

This double shock woke MAJ up to the new challenge caused by the 1935 Act. This was, after all, the rehearsal before the full self-government, which was to come. The Muslim League had to be reconstructed as a fighting electoral machine. In short, MAJ had to abandon his Liberal Constitutionalism, and follow MKG in what he had done to make the Congress a mass party. The experience MAJ had in the Central Legislature had value once. Now there was a new currency—of popular vote—which mattered.

MAJ then changed his tactics. The Muslim League had to become a street-fighting machine. Immediately, a hue and cry was raised that Congress governments in the provinces, especially UP, were oppressive as far as the Muslim minority was concerned. Congress atrocities had to be denounced. The singing of 'Vande Mataram' at official functions had to be objected to. Nehru had asked Congress to increase mass contact with Muslims. The League had to take a hostile stance.

Thus the reality of the prospect of self-government made the divisions between Hindus and Muslims, or rather, the Congress and the League, sharp and henceforward permanent. The old dreams of Hindu-Muslim unity, and the sharing of seats according to the

Lucknow formula, were now a thing of the past. The League had to distance Muslims from the Hindus if it was to win Muslim seats. The challenge to Jinnah was transparent. While MKG had retired, leaving the active leadership to the younger generation of Nehru, Patel and Prasad, MAJ was on his own. He did not have a ready team of younger Muslims to share the burden except Liaquat Ali, who was an aristocratic Muslim man. Jinnah had to secure the Muslim-majority provinces in the northwest of India where Iqbal had spotted a territory exclusively for a Muslim nation. He had to try and win over Bengal and Assam where there was a Muslim majority.

One difficulty which was not as yet foreseen was that while Muslims may have been a nation, they were not defined by religion alone. Bengal had a different culture with strong linguistic roots in the Bengali language. The northwest—Iqbal's Nation—was Urdu-speaking, and had connections farther west with the Arab countries. There was a similar distance among Hindus between North and South India, where there was a similar linguistic difference. But those issues were as yet dormant.

FIVE

CHECK AND MATE

Then, once again, as it had happened in the past, the international situation changed the opportunities and challenges for both MKG and MAJ. War was declared in Europe after the efforts of Chamberlain, the British prime minister, to broker peace with Hitler—the Munich Agreement—failed. Linlithgow, the viceroy, committed India to the side of the Allies in the war as it was his right and responsibility. The 1935 Act had not yielded federal control to Indians. But the Congress acted as it always did. It overplayed its hand. It argued that the viceroy should have consulted the people of India, i.e. the Congress, before committing India to the war. Normally an Empire-loyalist, MKG appeared to have missed a trick. He had retired to his ashram at Wardha (Sevagram or Seagaon), and was busy with his constructive agenda. He was disengaged, and Nehru seems to have jumped the gun. It turned out to be a serious error. A situation where the Empire was at war for a second time within 20 years was not the time to play a sulking game. Again, subsequent Congress historians argue that this was a bold gesture. But there are cogent grounds for believing that the Partition became more likely after this overweening gesture.

This was the prize of a lifetime for MAJ. Now he could play the Empire-loyalist—a role which MKG had hitherto played so effectively. Linlithgow, the new viceroy, liked MKG even less than Willingdon had done. He was happy to ignore MKG, and invite MAJ to confer on how he could secure the cooperation of the Muslim League during the war. Not only were Muslims from the northwestern parts of India heavily represented in the armed forces, but if Linlithgow could cut the Congress down a size or two, MAJ was not one to regret it.

When the Congress ministries resigned on 22 October 1939, Jinnah saw his chance. He declared 22 December 1939 as the Day of Deliverance. It was a sort of populist gesture he was learning to deploy. Instead of his normal style of forensic speeches in the Council chambers, he had to be a street fighter if he was to catch up with MKG and his style of agitation. MKG regretted the Day of Deliverance in *Harijan*.

The reply from MAJ was swift:

> There is much in your article which is the result of imagination. It is due partly to the fact that you are living a secluded life at Segaon and partly because all your thoughts and actions are guided by 'inner voice'. You have very little concern for realities or what may be termed by ordinary mortals 'practical politics'. I sometimes wonder what can be common between practical politics and yourself, between democracy and the dictator of a political organisation of which he is not even a 'four-anna' member. But that is I suppose because you do not consider the Congress worthy of your membership.[69]

This was an unusually catty letter from a man who had known his

---

[69]Sayyid, Matlubul Hasan, *Jinnah: A Political Study*, Shaikh Muhammad, Lahore, 1945.

counter-party well over 20 years, but was now losing his patience with the other man's style. He continued the argument now by confronting MKG and his religiosity, and the issue of a Muslim nation in India:

> Let me say again that India is not a nation, not a country. It is a subcontinent composed of nationalities, Hindus and Muslims being the two major nations. Today you deny that religion can be a main factor in determining a nation, but you yourself when asked what your motive in life was 'the thing that leads us to do what we do whether it was religious, or social or political', said 'Purely religious'.
>
> I do not know any religion apart from human activity. It provides a moral basis to all other activities which they would otherwise lack reducing life to a maze of 'sound and fury signifying nothing.'[70]

In a sense, you can still see that MAJ had hopes of MKG bringing his enormous moral authority to bear on his own side of the Hindu-Muslim question. So he continued in another communication:

> Is it too much to hope and expect that you might play your legitimate role and abandon your chase after a mirage? Events are moving fast, a campaign of polemics, or your weekly discourse in the *Harijan* on metaphysics, philosophy and ethics, or your peculiar doctrines regarding *khaddar*, *ahimsa*, and spinning are not going to win India's freedom. Action and statesmanship alone will help us in our forward

---

[70]Ibid., p. 657.

march. I believe that you might still rise to your stature in the service of our country and make your contribution towards leading India to contentment and happiness.[71]

The language is a mixture of friendliness, immense respect and some irritation—that here was a man who could move mountains if he tried, but was sitting in an ashram in the middle of nowhere, and pontificating about khaddar, rather than resolving the Hindu-Muslim question. The rhetoric is about the one country they both worked so hard to liberate. India is the central concern for MAJ. This may again surprise the present generation.

MAJ was getting bold to see himself once again as a crucial player like he used to be back in those earlier decades when they were together fighting for Hindu-Muslim unity. For MAJ, here at last was parity, for the first time since the Khilafat agitation, between him and MKG as an interlocutor of the viceroy. He crowed loudly about this change in his fortunes. The Congress, as usual, saw this as a divide-and-rule policy. Of course, had they been invited but not MAJ, it would not have been divide-and-rule. The Congress saw itself as the sole party of Indian independence. Yet it had initiated the process that was to end its monopoly over HMG's regard.

So, 1939 saw MAJ copy over from MKG two of his achievements—building the Muslim League into a mass party and becoming the viceroy's favourite. He had lost his hard-won seniority in the Congress and national politics since 1920 when MKG stormed the Congress, if not 1915 when he returned from South Africa. Now as the war intervened, providence smiled on MAJ. All he had to

---

[71]Ibid., p. 658.

do was become MKG sans God. Even at this stage, he could not pretend that his demands for a separate group of Muslim provinces had anything to do with religion. Muslims, as a minority at the all-India level, could constitute a territory as a nation. It was territory which defined the nation despite the fact that there would be Muslims living in Hindu-majority areas. Neither Jinnah nor Iqbal fully formulated their idea of a Muslim **nation** as a Muslim **nation-state**. At this juncture, the idea was not that it had to be separate from the Hindu nation-state, but that it had to be autonomous at least, with a weak Hindu-dominated Centre.

He did make some concessions, which showed that he had learnt a trick or two from MKG. So he began to wear the Muslim dress with *achkan*, *churidar*s and a beautiful turban during his political meetings. But it took him a bit more time before he would speak in Urdu. Some years later, when MKG wrote him a letter in Gujarati (with an Urdu translation), he replied in English saying it was 'the only language in which I make no mistake.'[72]

With Congress ministers having resigned from their ministries, the British were happy to induct politicians from other parties—the Hindu Mahasabha, the Muslim League, and even communists (after Hitler's attack on the Soviet Union)—to fill the ministries. MAJ went on a whirlwind tour to set up and strengthen Muslim League branches around the country. This was a heaven-sent opportunity as he could rouse Muslim anger by recounting Congress highhandedness while in power. He had to buttress the presence of the League in Punjab and Sind, where the ruling parties did not give a berth to the Muslim League.

Then in 1940, he made the bold move during a conference

---

[72]Ibid., p. 792.

of the Muslim League in Lahore to unfurl the Pakistan banner without so much as mentioning the name. He was a pleader par excellence. He argued a brief brilliantly. He was known in his chosen profession not as a great lawyer who could prepare a brief. He needed help for that.[73] Luckily for him, Iqbal had prepared the Pakistan brief. He had turned the routine and specialized demand for protection of Muslim minorities into a demand for territory for a Muslim nation. Jinnah now had a brilliant brief. Even more helpful to him was the passing away of Iqbal on the eve of the Lahore meeting. MAJ was now the only leader of sufficient seniority available to represent the Muslim nation. To establish his credentials, he had to dismiss the Muslim favouritism shown by Gandhi. It was not religion. It was a distinct nationhood that MAJ was fighting for.

The Pakistan demand was well orchestrated by MAJ. Given that out in the east there were two provinces—Bengal and Assam—which the League could claim as Muslim-majority provinces, Jinnah turned his charm on Fazlul Huq who was the leader of the Krishak Praja Party of Bengal, a peasants' party interested in land reforms. So he let Fazlul Huq move the motion specifying the demand that the four Muslim-majority provinces in the northwest plus Bengal and Assam in the east be considered as a separate grouping. This Lahore Resolution has gone down in history as the demand for Pakistan, which brought Partition nearer.

Of course, MAJ and everyone else had only the vaguest notion of what the grouping of the four Muslim-majority provinces in the northwest plus the two in the northeast would do to the shape of independent India. But as of now, no exchange of population

---

[73]Bolitho, Hector, *Jinnah: Creator of Pakistan*, John Murray, London, 1954, p. 17.

or division of assets was contemplated. The idea was that within a Federation such as the one proposed in the 1935 Act, there would be subgroups of states within a region, which would pool their sovereignty together and behave like a quasi-independent part of the nation. The final Constitution had yet to be drawn up by Indian leaders, once the British Parliament passed the next big grant of self-government. Nobody was certain, but a sort of West Pakistan, East Pakistan and Hindustan would coexist in an independent India.

MAJ was working away on yet another version of what he still believed was an updated version of his Lucknow 1916 programme of Hindu-Muslim unity. Now he conceded that MKG was the senior partner in this venture. So he wrote:

> Mr. Gandhi's notion of justice is to follow what he advises then alone it can be right. I am constrained to say I wish Mr. Gandhi will stop airing views which change from day to day and week to week and which consistently perpetuate inconsistencies and apply his mind to the only and one question, namely settling the Hindu-Muslim question as he, of all Congress leaders is best fitted to represent the Hindus as such and he can deliver the goods on behalf of the Hindus and bring about a complete adjustment between the two major communities and the rest will follow. I need hardly reiterate that I am willing to help to the utmost of my power on behalf of the Muslims towards an honourable solution.[74]

Congress was drifting. Having resigned from the ministries, and getting nothing in return from the viceroy, MKG tried a

---

[74]Ibid., p. 673.

series of individual satyagrahas declaring peaceful disobedience. Vinoba Bhave was chosen as the first satyagrahi, followed by Nehru. Both of them were *brahmachari*, according to Gandhi. Jawaharlal, now a widower, also qualified as a brahmachari! (MKG never quite understood extramarital sexual relations!) But again, the government took no notice, and the movement fizzled out. Surprisingly for him, MKG was failing to read the minds of the British correctly. The government of India was busy helping the war effort. It expected loyalty.

The War Comes to India

Then again, the international context changed, this time offering the Congress a reprieve. Hitler launched his Operation Barbarossa attacking the Soviet Union in June 1941, in breach of the Molotov-Ribbentrop Pact. Later in December 1941, Japan attacked Pearl Harbor outside Hawaii islands, which were part of US territory. At last, the Americans would join the war on the British side, and the Soviet Union would join the Allies. This would be a proper World War, east and west, north and south. The British were happy as they were no longer alone in Europe, fighting the Germans. What they had not reckoned with was Japanese strength in Southeast Asia.

Singapore fell to the Japanese, and the war came closer to India. Instead of a source of supply of war material and soldiers, India looked like becoming a target for the Japanese. This was as early as February 1942. With the Americans insisting that Churchill be seen to be doing something about India, Stafford Cripps was sent to India to explore whether the Congress and other Indian leaders could be harnessed into the war effort. Neither Churchill nor Linlithgow wanted Cripps to promise too much. If he was seen to be failing due to Congress intransigence, his mission would succeed as far as Churchill was concerned. But then, as coalition partners, the Labour Party did not want Cripps to fail, though Attlee thought he was too far left.

Cripps did not have much to offer to the Indians in wartime. They would be inducted on the Viceroy's Executive Council. But again, the Congress wanted more. It wanted to be treated like a cabinet and wanted the defence portfolio. As the Congress had no expertise in defence, and Auchinlek, as the commander-in-chief, would not give up his post, there was no go. The only advantage for Jinnah was that he was treated with much greater respect than before. He knew that all he had to do was to appear agreeable to the offer. He knew that the Congress would reject it, and earn the opprobrium. Gandhi was, as usual, not officially a part of the Congress delegation but was invited in a personal capacity. As Cripps could only promise a self-government offer after the end of the war, Gandhi dismissed it as 'a post-dated cheque'. Some journalist needlessly added 'on a failing bank'. That was the end of the Cripps Mission.

The Americans could see that tackling the India question would not be easy. But it was not urgent either. It could wait till after the Allied victory. In 1942, the Pacific War had just started, and Hitler was progressing towards Moscow. The Congress had its internationalist concerns, mainly thanks to Nehru, but its focus was its own priorities. The British, like the Americans, decided Congress could wait.

But somehow, MKG, who had taken a backseat since 1934,

decided to force the issue. This was a surprising move as he had left the active work to the new team consisting of Nehru and Patel. But he made a bold move. This was his final push, his final version of the Khilafat movement manoeuvre. He let it be known that he was offering one more chance to Linlithgow to negotiate, or he would launch a Civil Disobedience movement. He did send feelers via Meeraben (Madeleine Slade), who was his principal British follower and had defence connections in her family background. But Linlithgow was not playing.

Then MKG said he would launch his Quit India call on 8 August 1942 at the Bombay conference of the Congress. Nehru was not sure it would work, nor was Maulana Azad, the then Congress president. But others, like Sardar Patel and Rajendra Prasad, always followed MKG blindly. The government took no chances, and arrested the leaders the night before the launch of the Quit India movement. The Congress leadership spent the next three years in jail. This was the second gift MAJ got from the Congress. Now he had more time to prove how helpful he could be to HMG in time of war.

So while MKG was in the Aga Khan Palace near Poona, and the Congress leadership was being treated as Class 1 prisoners in the Ahmednagar Fort (Nehru was busy writing what became his best-known book *The Discovery of India*), MAJ was out organizing and recruiting for his party. Even so, he was aware that they were all just in the waiting room till the train arrived for the journey ahead. Thus, in a speech in Delhi in April 1943, MAJ said:

> I say to the Hindus—and the British know it better than any body else—that the quickest way for the freedom of the people, both Hindus and Muslims, is Pakistan. It may come in

my life time or not, you will remember these words of mine.

Nobody would welcome it more than myself if Mr. Gandhi is even now willing to come to a settlement with the Muslim League on the basis of Pakistan. Let me tell you, it will be the greatest day both for the Hindus and Mussalmans. If he has made up his mind, what is there to prevent Mr. Gandhi from writing direct to me? He is writing to the Viceroy, why does he not write to me direct?

But I do not see evidence of any kind of change of policy on the part of Mr. Gandhi or Congress or the Hindu leadership.[75]

It was Dr Ambedkar who was still angry about being compelled by Gandhi to give up his separate votes for the untouchables. There was some attempt by Jinnah to get together with two 'Hindu' dissident leaders—Dr Ambedkar and the Periyar Ramasami Naicker, but nothing came of it. Dr Ambedkar lashed out at both Gandhi and Jinnah in January 1943:

...it would be difficult to find two personalities, who rival Mr. Gandhi and Mr. Jinnah in their colossal egotism, to whom personal ascendancy is everything, and the country's cause a mere counter on the table. They have made Indian politics into matters of personal feud, and the consequences hold no terrors for them. Between them, Indian politics would become frozen, and no political action would be possible. Their feelings of supremacy and infallibility is [sic] strengthened by the Indian Press. Indian journalism today is written by drummer boys to glorify their heroes. Never

---

[75]Ibid., p. 791.

has the interest of a country been sacrificed so senselessly for the propaganda of hero worship.[76]

After Cripps, the Congress was now sure that whatever the Americans might say, only the British would decide. They knew the Labour Party was friendly to them. Even in jail, they were being treated royally. They were just waiting for the next call to govern. However, Gandhi suffered a double loss. First, his long-time secretary Mahadev Desai died soon after entering the Aga Khan Palace. Then Kasturba, his wife and companion since their childhood, died on 22 February 1944 after 61 years of marriage. For this last journey, she had got herself arrested knowing that her husband would be too. It shattered him. Of all his friends and followers, she was the one he had known the longest. She had transformed herself and her life, following him wherever he took himself. At the end, she expressed the wish that she wanted to be wrapped in yarn spun by him. It was a true expression of her love for the difficult boy she had marred in her childhood. She became known as 'Baa', mother of the nation.

From then on, he was truly a lonely man.

(It is not germane to my theme, but it is remarkable how many of the leaders of the Indian independence movement were widowers—Jinnah, Nehru, Patel, and now Gandhi.)

Gandhi was released early, due to his frail condition. Not missing a chance, Jinnah met Gandhi at his Malabar Hill house for a dialogue in September 1944. Again, Gandhi proposed that they talk in Gujarati, but Jinnah knew a trap when it was yawning in

---

[76]Guha, Ramachandra, *Gandhi: The Years that Changed the World: 1914–1918*, Penguin Random House, Gurgaon, 2018, p. 689.

front of him. The Gandhi-Jinnah dialogue did not get anywhere. Gandhi would not claim to represent the Congress, nor would he concede that the Congress spoke only for the Hindus. He also failed to grant Jinnah's contention that the Muslim League was the sole body representing Muslims.

That was not new. After all, these two knew each other pretty thoroughly. What, however, Gandhi saw in Jinnah's Lahore Resolution was a restricted plebiscite on who decided the extent of Pakistan. Gandhi said that the plebiscite should be voted upon by all the citizens of the Muslim-majority provinces by district. This meant that a province, despite having a Muslim majority, might have significant areas with non-Muslim majority. Thus, Jinnah's partition proposals could be accepted only if they led to further division at the district level, rather than just at the level of the province with only the Muslims voting.

Here again, howsoever eccentric Gandhi sounded and howsoever evasive about his own power within the Congress, he had grasped the essential idea that not just entire provinces could be traded, but subdivisions within provinces. He preferred an undivided and free India. But if it came to the point that India could be independent only if it was divided, he would save every bit of India he could hold on to. Punjab and Bengal were to be divided if Jinnah got his Pakistan. This was clever, as Jinnah realized. He was going to get 'a moth-eaten' Pakistan. Gandhi proved that when it came to thinking ahead of the practicalities of setting up two sovereign states out of British India, he had been far too perceptive. And indeed, although everyone calls what happened in August 1947 the Partition of India, actually the Gandhi formula was accepted, and only Punjab and Bengal were partitioned in an east-west fashion, not all of India. This, of course, meant a much more bloody process as people moved across boundaries, but the minorities left behind in these provinces which formed Pakistan were very much minimal.

When the 'nations' of Jinnah's statement became nation-states, the consequences were as catastrophic as they were unexpected by the leaders. The division of Punjab and Bengal did happen. What happened next should not have surprised the decision-makers. Legally, no human movement across the boundaries of the two nation-states were necessary. Dr Ambedkar, who studied the human movements in Europe after the end of the empires in Europe in 1918, knew well how it would turn out. But no one paid any attention to what he wrote. Even Mountbatten (who had become viceroy by March 1947), no less than all the London-trained barristers, Gandhi, Jinnah, Patel, Nehru, was surprised that people had to move across: Muslims from east to west Punjab, and from west to east Bengal, and Hindus from east to west Bengal, and from west to east Punjab. Hindu Sindhis had to move south to the Bombay Province from which they had been separated not long ago. But that was yet in the unknown future. (These leaders were like all leaders—somewhat cut off from the lives and thinking of ordinary people. Even Gandhi, however ordinarily he might have clothed himself.)

Another issue was when such a move would take place. Could the principal parties arrive at an understanding of how the Constitution was to be written by the British Parliament to legislate? There had been an idea that a Federation with strong autonomous provinces and a weak Centre with minimal powers would be proposed. The other idea was that the British Parliament itself would legislate, and guarantee Muslim minority rights before granting independence.

The difference would be that a weak Centre and powerful provinces, combined with regional groupings, could be set up without creating two sovereign states. In a way, the 1935 Act was suitable for one federation with powerful regional groups. But, of course, no agreement could be reached before the British government made its move.

Endgame

The war got over with an Allied victory. It was followed by general elections in the UK, which returned a Labour government with a thumping majority. Indian independence was a priority for the Labour Party. It was written in the manifesto of the party. Prime Minister Attlee was someone who had been on the Simon Commission. It was clear that the question of India was urgent. Attlee was in favour of dispatch, although Wavell, as viceroy, thought they would have to stretch out their stay.

Elections were held again for the provinces and the Central Legislative Assembly. Jinnah's hard work in organizing the Muslim League paid off as the latter won 428 out of 482 Muslim seats, and all reserved Muslim seats for the Central Legislative Assembly. It was clear that the Muslim League could claim to speak for Muslims. But Jinnah still had anxieties. He wanted the British to deliver guarantees for the Muslim minority, rather than leave it for the newly elected representatives who would write the Constitution.

Two moves were made. A Cabinet Mission was sent with

Cripps, Lord Pethick-Lawrence and Alexander to discuss the future constitutional arrangements. This mission more or less delivered what was wanted. They proposed that the provinces be grouped into three separate bunches. The four northwestern provinces were one group. The northeastern provinces, Bengal and Assam were another group. In the middle would be a large number of Hindu-majority provinces where the Congress had won.

In one way, the Cabinet Mission squared the circle. There would be an undivided India as the Congress wished, with three groups of provinces, including two Muslim-majority groups which were what Jinnah wanted for his Pakistan. So there would be an all-India Federation with a weak Centre and almost autonomous provinces—free to form subgroups as Jinnah had wanted. The provinces, individually or as groups, had to hand over the responsibility for defence, finance and foreign policy to the Centre. Jinnah was happy to accept this settlement even before the Congress did.

Gandhi saw that there would be the recently elected body at the Centre with a Congress majority which doubled as the Constituent Assembly for the new Federation. Knowing the rules of British Parliament, Gandhi saw that the Congress could modify the regional grouping, and write the Constitution it wished to. He also sensed that this might alarm Jinnah when he realized what he had agreed to. He conveyed his views to the Cabinet Mission, but as it was his day of silence, the message was hard to decipher. But Cripps's biographer described it as follows: 'The language was metaphorical: the light in the darkness had vanished leaving a vacuum. Gandhi admitted that while "I must not act against my instinct, he had nothing tangible to prove that there were danger signals".[77]

Nehru also realized what Gandhi had discovered. His knowledge of British parliamentary practice was equally sharp. Now that Jinnah had agreed, the Congress had him where they wanted. But Nehru was not one for subtle messages. So when asked at a press conference as to whether the Congress agreed to the Cabinet Mission proposals, Nehru asserted the British tradition that a new Parliament cannot be bound by decisions of earlier bodies. 'Congress would be unfettered by agreements and free to meet all situations as they arise.' (It was Maulana Azad who had just handed over the Congress presidency over to Nehru, who revealed how crucial this statement was to the outcome of the process.) This was much disputed when his book *India Wins Freedom* came out in 1959. Recently, in April 2023, the Congress Party removed any mention of Azad from its galaxy of great Congress leaders of the past.[78]

This was on 10 July 1946. The Cabinet Mission had left satisfied that they got the agreement of all parties. Jinnah immediately saw that he was trapped. He had agreed to the plan, but the power to undo it remained with the Congress majority in the Constituent Assembly. Jinnah then did something he had never, ever done in the whole of his political career. He deployed the weapon of 'direct action' as he had seen Gandhi do in those early days, soon after his arrival back in India—the protests against the Rowlatt Acts, and then all the way to the Khilafat movement. This was what

---

[77]Desai, Meghnad, *The Rediscovery of India*, Penguin Random House, Gurgaon, India, 2009, p. 254.
[78]Ibid., p. 256.

had made Jinnah lose his exalted position in the Congress. He had deplored Gandhi's tactics then. But now, he had no time to reopen negotiations. So he abandoned his constitutionalist ways and went the way of disobedience. He declared a Direct Action Day on 16 August 1946. Gandhi saw the danger immediately: 'We are not in the midst of Civil War. But we are nearing it.' Yet Gandhi kept on hoping that he could talk Jinnah out of his demand for a separate sovereign state. As he said, 'I claim to have his [Jinnah's] friendship. After all, he also belongs to India. Whatever happens, I have to spend my life with him.'[79]

But it was too late. The switch in Jinnah's tactics—from constitutional discussions to (somewhat) uncivil disobedience—was the last thing anyone had expected. That proved to be the magic bullet, in a literal as well as figurative sense. The carefully crafted Cabinet Mission Plan had to be abandoned. What followed over the next 11 months has been well described in great detail. It was an ironic paradox as much as a tragic outcome. After a 30-year-long, albeit troubled, partnership—often on opposite sides, but always fighting for Indian independence—Jinnah succeeded in his plan by using his version of disobedience of the law, which he learnt from Gandhi. Gandhi failed in his dream of achieving Hindu-Muslim unity, and an undivided India. Jinnah was not troubled by having to instruct the crowd to be nonviolent. But then he knew from the old days in Bombay that such appeals for nonviolence were never obeyed. So he abandoned his Liberal Constitutionalism in his final throw of the dice.

The riots and murders that followed over the next few months

---

[79]Gandhi, Gopal, *The Oxford Gandhi: Essential Writings*, Oxford University Press, New Delhi, 2008, p. 502.

led to a last-minute revision of the plan. Attlee had understood that there had to be a change. Wavell was trying to put together a sort of cabinet with the Congress and the Muslim League sharing ministries. As usual, MAJ had insisted that only the League could nominate Muslims, which the Congress would not agree to. After much to-ing and fro-ing, an interim government was arrived at. For such things, Gandhi would not bother to give his view. It was Nehru who was now the de facto prime minister Jinnah had to negotiate with. Nehru had no respect for Jinnah, and never understood the appeal of religion.

There was a meeting back in London in December 1946, where Nehru and Jinnah met with the Labour Cabinet. Wavell had gone back to offer his view. Attlee saw that he needed to replace Wavell, and choose a new viceroy. He chose Mountbatten, who had performed well as a naval chief in Southeast Asia, fighting the Japanese. Mountbatten had royal blood in him, and a charming wife Edwina who was the daughter of a multimillionaire. Nehru had met them during his visit to Singapore.

Mountbatten agreed to be viceroy, but demanded plenipotentiary powers so he could make decisions rapidly without having to refer back to London. He became the last and only viceroy to get such powers. As soon as he arrived in March 1947, he talked to the principal parties, and decided that there was no chance of implementing the Cabinet Mission proposals.

Gandhi made a somewhat strange proposal that Jinnah be given the chance to form the government as he liked. By this time, the urgency of the matter was such that Nehru refused to support this peculiar solution. Gandhi had figured that despite being in charge of the executive, the Congress majority in the

Constituent Assembly or Parliament would restrain Jinnah. But then, Jinnah could see the trap just as well.

From here on, within a fortnight of his arrival, Mountbatten took Nehru and Patel in confidence to convince them that the Partition was the only solution. By this time, Nehru and Patel had taken charge of the Congress, and were, in effect, in the Cabinet as prime minister and home minister. Gandhi was out touring riot-torn areas, and was out of the loop. So the decision to accept the Partition was not even conveyed to Gandhi immediately. Mountbatten flew back to London despite having plenipotentiary powers. This was the final decision to be approved by the Cabinet.

Mountbatten came back armed with the Cabinet's approval. Gandhi found out about this at a Congress meeting, where no one objected to it except for a young Ram Manohar Lohia. Even Maulana Azad kept quiet, just smoking away.

The die was cast. There would not be one Federation with a weak Centre and autonomous provinces grouped together. There would be two sovereign nation-states—India and Pakistan. Pakistan was created by following what Gandhi had told Jinnah in their last talks in Bombay in September 1944. Voting had to be done by the majorities as well as the minorities in each district through their legislative assemblies. However knowledgeable Jinnah was in constitutional methods, Gandhi proved to be the more astute one in judging how that decision would be shaped by the British. Gandhi proved to be the better constitutionalist. But then, Jinnah had used the Gandhian weapon of direct action to secure the result he had been fighting for.

Even so, they kept on meeting till the final days in May 1947, before Partition was finally announced on 2 June 1947, along with the day of Independence, which would be on 15 August 1947. In a joint statement issued at the request of Lord Mountbatten, the viceroy, Gandhi and Jinnah, the two most senior politicians in the Indian independence movement, said:

> We deeply deplore the recent acts of lawlessness and violence that have brought about the utmost disgrace on the fair name of India. We denounce for all time the use of force to achieve political ends and we call upon all the communities of India to whatever persuasion they belong not only to refrain from all acts of violence and disorder, but also to avoid in speech and writing any words which might've considered an incitement to such acts.[80]

But Gandhi, in his heart of hearts, knew better. He had said to his son Devdas, 'An Englishman will not be argued into yielding; he only yields under compulsion of events.'[81]

So the two Gujarati, England-returned barristers laboured all their adult years trying to win self-government for India, their common birthplace. But, in the attempt, they achieved something that was not quite what they had intended. Gandhi was hailed as 'father of the nation', but it was less of a nation than he had known all his life. Jinnah too missed the nation he had fought so hard for, but created a wholly new nation—Pakistan, a 'moth-eaten' version of what he had bid for.

Gandhi was not one to celebrate independence. Of course, the younger generation of Nehru and even Patel had kept him

---

[80]Ibid., p. 512.
[81]Ibid.

out of the loop in the final stages when they signed up to the two-nation solution (which, of course, they later denied ever doing, blaming Jinnah, the British and everyone else). But Gandhi was still of the older vintage. He still thought of India as it was till 13 August 1947, before either Pakistan or India were born as separate nation-states.

So when there was a move by the new government of India to withhold Pakistan's share of the cash available in the coffers of British India—around ₹55 crore—he went on a fast, his ultimate weapon. This was regardless of the news that there was an invasion of Jammu and Kashmir from the Pakistan side. MKG was not against India defending its newly demarcated territory, but he was not going to tolerate reneging on due payment.

That proved to be his last fast. Though he did not have to fast for long as his followers, now in power, immediately paid up, there were ugly reverberations now. Partition had hurt the Hindu nationalists. They had not liked Gandhi and his Hinduism ever since the Khilafat movement. They wanted, as he of course also did, an *Akhand Hindustan*, an undivided (British) India. But now, after Partition, there were two pieces of it—Muslim Pakistan and one that would be India.

Not even six months had gone by since Independence. The nation-states, which were once a single nation, had to be seen as eternal enemies. Nathuram Godse, who assassinated Gandhi on 30 January 1948, and immediately surrendered himself to the police, was not a 'madman' or a 'terrorist', though without doubt his deed was heinous. He did not deny his guilt. He did, however, make a long statement—around a hundred pages in print—in the court. It contained a critique of MKG's policies in a section called 'Gandhiji's Politics X rayed'.[82] You may or may not (as I do not) agree with it. But it examined various moves by MKG over the years—from 1915 when he came back from South Africa, till Independence.

Savarkar, whom MKG had met in London back in 1909 and disagreed with, was implicated in this trial but was acquitted. But it was Savarkar's Maharashtrian 'muscular' Hinduism, as against Gandhi's Gujarati Vaishnavite or Jain Hinduism, which clashed on 30 January 1948. Gandhi had innovated the satyagraha, a weapon for the powerless fighting the powerful, but nonviolently. But ahimsa, as I argued above, is Buddhist or Jain and not a part of Sanatan Dharma. Savarkar and Godse's Hinduism was based on the memories of Shivaji fighting the Mughal armies back in the seventeenth century. Godse cited the Ramayana and the Gita as evidence which illustrated killing your enemy—Rama killing Ravana and Arjuna being told by Krishna to fight—as sanctioned by Hinduism.

Hinduism is, after all, not like Christianity—a monolithic religion with a definite theology. It is a rich feast of which different regions with different histories and languages have partaken. Gandhi had his Hinduism and his assailant had his. In recent years, while Gandhi is still saluted as Father of the Nation, it is Savarkar whose Hinduism has won.

Whatever the future of Gandhi's Hinduism, there is no doubt that his 'constructive programme'—rural uplift, anti-Western modernity, spinning and khadi, not to say his admonition that the Congress should dissolve itself and not become a ruling

---

[82]Godse, Gopal, and Nathuram Godse, *Why I Assassinated Gandhi*, Farsight Publishers and Distributors, Delhi, 2020, pp. 46–82.

party, have all been forgotten. He is the Father of the Nation, remembered twice a year, but not much more. His message has helped struggles for justice and equality abroad, but he is just a smiling face from a currency note in India. Gandhi endures, but Gandhism is forgotten. His eager followers—Gandhians—in his ashrams had become an object of mirth within 25 years of his death.[83]

Jinnah died within 13 months of getting his Pakistan. He had been ailing for quite a while, at least five years if not longer. In 1944, his doctors diagnosed a problem in his lungs. Jinnah had been, for most of his adult life, a tall thin man who smoked regularly. In those days, people were not aware of the costs of smoking in terms of health. But his illness remained a secret. It is not clear whether the British knew about the threat to his health, but if so, they did not take advantage of it. In 1946, when Wavell was trying to put together a 'Cabinet' from the members of Congress and the League, Jinnah was diagnosed as suffering from bronchitis and lung troubles. Dr Jal Patel, his specialist adviser, said, 'There is the petulance that goes with the illness Jinnah was suffering from.' Then again in March 1947, Jinnah was reported to have had a nervous breakdown. The strain was supposed to have been caused by his trip along with Nehru to London to discuss a last-minute compromise before Independence. Alan Campbell, who was Mountbatten's aide, wrote in his *Mission with Mountbatten*: 'Jinnah was seventy; already an old man and slowly dying.'[84]

Flying from Delhi to Karachi on 7 August 1947, MAJ said, 'I suppose this is the last time I'll be looking at Delhi. That is

---

[83]Mehta, Ved, *Mahatma Gandhi and His Apostles*, Penguin, London, 1977.

[84]Bolitho, Hector, *Jinnah: Creator of Pakistan*, John Murray, London, 1954, p. 178.

the end of that'. He is supposed to have said to his Naval ADC Lt. Ahsan, 'Do you know I never expected to see Pakistan in my lifetime. We have to be grateful to God for what we have achieved.'

Here then is the ending paradox. Gandhi, the apostle of nonviolence, died a violent death at the hands of a fellow Hindu. Jinnah, a nonreligious Liberal Constitutionalist, all his life fought for, and created, a nation-state for a minority defined by religion. But he died peacefully having declared his gratitude to God for making him a success.

Invoking God was MKG's speciality, not MAJ's. But he had not changed much. The day before the formal birth of his Pakistan, he said in the Pakistan Constituent Assembly that Pakistan would welcome people of all religions. He might have fought for the rights of Muslim-majority provinces, but now that he had won what he bid for, he revealed himself, to the surprise of his Hindu detractors and Muslim friends, as an advocate of Hindu-Muslim unity, and a secular Liberal Constitutionalist.

Muhammad Ali Jinnah died on 11 September 1948, at 10.20 p.m.

They both lost the Old India which they loved so much, and worked so hard to liberate from British rule.

How and why?

An Epic Failure

More than 76 years on, it may have come as a surprise to many readers to read of Jinnah talking about his desire to free India from foreign rule. We have irretrievably lost that Old India which both these English barristers from Gujarat loved so much.

They tried their best and longer than any other two people to save India, and lost. Of course, by the time they lost, younger people had moved in to the front. Their patience was wearing thin. They wanted executive power to change their beloved countries for the better. They were all getting old and tired, and wanted an end to the bickering, as Nehru said to Leonard Mosley.

But, in a way, while the Nehru generation was impatient for power, and wanted a territory over which they would have effective dominion (in order to modernize and enrich the country), the older generation had a sentimental commitment. Gandhi and Jinnah were only a decade or two older than Nehru, but they had grown up during a solid Victorian Age. It may be heretical to say so nowadays, but their ancestors had never witnessed such tranquillity across the vast subcontinent. India got its borders defined, and a single monarch's rule over its entire territory, for the first time in its history only after 1858 (which is why India's borders have British names—Durand, Radcliffe, MacMahon, etc.). The generation of Mohan and Muhammad was almost the first to be born in that Undivided India. For them, it was the only India they knew.

But they had also been affected by Macaulay's injection of an education in English. This, in turn, gave them notions of nation and of self-rule. It was reinforced when they went to the mother country of the Empire. The patriotic song was 'Rule Britannia', with that enticing line:

'Britons never, never shall be slaves.'

That line, asserting a liking for freedom, became known all over the British Empire over the next century. But it began with India and its aspirations. In Europe, the mid-century revolution of 1848 had been a demand for responsible kingdoms. Bismarck had seized the moment and built the German Reich from a motley collection of monarchies and dukedoms, with Prussia in the lead. The Italian struggle for freedom, with Mazzini as hero, was popular, as was the Irish freedom movement. Empires broke up after the First World War, and Europe became a (quarrelsome) family of nations. Nations were identified with territory—Greece, Italy, Poland, Hungary. Gandhi and Jinnah were the young men eager to emulate Europe, and fight for independence.

Given that they were subjects of an Empire which was a unique combination of monarchy and democracy, their expectations of building a free India were shot through with ideas of democracy and elections, and parliamentary procedures. In 1857, the sepoys might have risen to restore the Mughal Emperor, but for the new generation born under Victoria, India, when free, was not going to be a kingdom. It was going to be a democracy won over from the Empire using the constitutional method that they had imbibed in London.

This trajectory was Jinnah's preferred choice almost till the end. It proved inadequate, because in a democracy numbers matter, and he discovered that going by the British way of looking at India, there were at least two subject groups there—Hindus and Muslims. Despite the introduction of separate electorates by his favourite Liberal Party, Jinnah chose to unite the two streams as his first option. Gandhi got his induction into democracy in a much more hostile environment—Natal and the Transvaal. The Boers were not a conquered nation, but nor were they free. They disliked the British, and denied them full voting rights in Transvaal as they denied these to Asian immigrants and native

Black Africans. His fight was for getting his clients registered as proper subjects of the Queen Empress. He was forced to take up the cudgels on behalf of all Indian immigrants, rich and poor, Hindus and Muslims, Gujaratis, Biharis and Tamils. He had to agitate to secure their recognition as subjects.

The duality of patient constitutionalism and direct action agitation defined the two paths taken up by Jinnah and Gandhi. It was like a game of snakes and ladders as to who was ahead, and who jumped over to go past his friend and rival. At the moment of Gandhi's return to India from South Africa in 1915, Jinnah was ahead, though Gandhi had acquired a name for himself, thanks to his activities in South Africa. Then the Rowlatt Acts and the Jallianwala Bagh agitations took Gandhi ahead of Jinnah. The Gandhian tactics of civil disobedience clothed in Hindu religious symbolism were not Jinnah's cup of tea. So he slid further back, and while Gandhi became the undisputed leader of the Congress Party, now a mass political movement, Jinnah stuck to the constitutionalist path. Chauri Chaura shattered Hindu-Muslim unity, and strengthened the Hindu Mahasabha. The Motilal Nehru Report shut Jinnah out. He exited India, and went back to London.

The 1935 Act called him back for parliamentary elections, and he realized that the Muslim League was ill-equipped to fight the Congress, even for the Muslim seats. So he had to become a street-fighting politician. Luckily for him, war broke out, and the Congress overplayed its hand. He was back in the favour of the British government in India. Gandhi dropped out of active membership or leadership of the party. Congress and Gandhi were shunted out of the way through the war. Jinnah was the sole politician talking with the British rulers about the shape of things to come. Jinnah was lucky that Iqbal found a formula to transform the parliamentary contest between Hindus and Muslims into a battle for nationhood.

The Congress, now effectively led by Nehru, was baffled and incredulous. Jawaharlal had a problem understanding the hold of religion on people. He had imbibed a simple version of Marxism which told him that every social problem had an economic base. So he attributed the Hindu-Muslim differences to economic problems such as desire for jobs among Muslims. He also underestimated Jinnah as a minor part of the independence movement, not realizing that Jinnah had made this a struggle for independence as well as a redefinition of what the nation was that was demanding independence. By the time Nehru became dominant on the independence front, Jinnah had lost his previous senior position. But, of course, Jinnah was to regain it.

Again, the battle was transformed by America's entry into the war, and its insistence that Britain grant self-rule to India. So the Congress acquired outside support while the Allied forces were grateful for the performance of the Indian Army. But, unusually for him, Gandhi overplayed his hand, and launched the Quit India Movement. The Congress was a twice loser as its leadership spent the next three years in jail, while the younger generation reproduced a Chauri Chaura-style violent movement. That agitation was suppressed. The balance of strength was even as between Congress for Hindus and Muslim League for Muslims, who were, of course, yet a minority in an all-India context. Then, luckily there was victory for the Allies, and for the Labour Party in the British elections. It came to power determined to help the Congress further.

The choice then was a Federation with a weak Centre and powerful provinces, with a Parliament acting as a Constituent Assembly to draft the Constitution of New India. This would have a built-in Hindu majority. Without the British pre-guarantee of Muslim rights, Jinnah was unwilling to play. He was granted regions in the northwest and northeast, so he agreed. Then he discovered, as Gandhi and Nehru did, that the power would be in the Constituent Assembly where the Congress or the Hindus would have a majority, with no binding constraints from any previous treaty.

By this time, it was too late to reopen negotiations. Attlee indicated his decision to leave by July 1948. Jinnah struck out, and launched his direct action plan for 16 August 1946. As during the Khilafat agitation, the Indian crowd behaved predictably, and months of killings followed. This hastened the final solution. It started with separate electorates, and ended with separate sovereign nation-states.

The Irish Parallel

What was interesting about this debate was that while it was going on, no one seemed to have cited (to my knowledge) the Irish experience. Superficially, it has been said (perhaps only since the Partition of India) that the British always caused the nations they colonized to break up once they left. Ireland and India are, of course, prime examples. The Irish case must have been known since 1922 when the Irish Free State was created while the Ulster province stayed in the UK. The major area of Ireland—the Catholic or Nationalist area—became independent by acquiring home rule and the unionists in Belfast stayed inside the United Kingdom. So this was a half-Partition, and it was blatantly engineered by Sir Edward Carson, MP, and the Conservative Party, in defiance of the Liberal government which had been willing to grant the Irish home rule before 1914. Then, of course, the war intervened and the rest is history.

The Irish division was sectarian, i.e. within the Christians as to Catholics or Nationalists, who were the majority, and Unionists who were Protestant. Geographically, there was a clear division as the Unionists were (are) in the north-east of Ireland, while the rest of Ireland was Catholic. The interesting part of this story is how the Catholic minority in Northern Ireland fought against the discrimination they were suffering from the Unionist majority during the decades that followed. This fight was violent on both sides, and lasted from the late 1960s to the 1990s. It was the time of the Troubles, as these years were called. Peace and an end to violent conflict were negotiated in 1998 (thanks again to a Labour-majority government in the UK), with American intervention (again), and a Good Friday Agreement was signed between the Irish Republic, the United Kingdom and the Belfast government to have peace and no hard border between the two parts of Ireland. The Irish Republic agreed to drop the pledge in its Constitution to regain the six counties which formed Northern Ireland. The novel thing about this agreement was that each community—Catholics and Protestants—had to vote on the Good Friday Agreement separately and approve it with a majority in each community. This overcame the disadvantage of Catholics being a permanent minority in a democratic regime, with no special rights. Governments in Northern Ireland had to be across both communities. (As I was writing this in April 2023, President Biden was in Belfast celebrating the 25th anniversary of the Good Friday Agreement.)

It would be fanciful to think that at this late stage, Pakistan and India, with or without Bangladesh, could negotiate even a soft border or a free trade treaty. But the point of the story is that if voting on certain important topics was cast in a way that each community had to approve by a majority within the community before the proposal became a binding law, Muslim anxieties could have been assuaged. But in those early days, such 'consociational' voting arrangements were not known of.

SIX

TO THE POINT OF NO RETURN

CCould It Have Been Avoided?

It is always worth asking the counterfactual question. We know what happened. Once it has happened, there are cogent arguments to explain why it did. But these are often ex-post rationalizations. Could it have been otherwise? The Congress explanation has been to blame the entire episode of the Partition on Jinnah and the League, and their insistence on the two-nation theory, which the Congress claims it rejected. Add to that the perfidious Albion who had always believed in and practised divide-and-rule. Thus everyone was at fault but the Congress, which claims it had fought a nonviolent campaign for Indian independence from the onset of the Noncooperation Movement in 1922 under Gandhi's leadership. It is arguable, however, that the campaign was not nonviolent, whatever the Mahatma might have thought. From his call after Jallianwala Bagh to the Khilafat campaign, as he himself said, he seemed to have disregarded God's warning and tolerated bazaar violence. The Salt Satyagraha was peaceful, though it did not improve the chances of independence; what it did do was make Gandhi a figure known across the world. Film news documentaries had just arrived, and the sight of a frail, brown man walking miles across the Indian countryside became well known. Gandhi was featured on the cover of *Time* magazine, and became a celebrity in the USA.

The 1942 Quit India call was a damp squib compared to what he had hoped, and after the arrest of the Congress leadership, the mob broke out in violence. It was an unarmed struggle, not a nonviolent one. Of course, there were other groups which fought armed campaigns, but they have not been given their due by Congress historians. Gandhi's practice of nonviolence as a remedy for problems was demonstrated during the months before Independence as Hindu-Muslim riots broke out. In Calcutta, Noakhali and Bihar, he single-handedly brought peace and reconciliation, walking miles and defying all sorts of threats. This was Gandhi at his best when British India was at its worst. Undiluted and away from assorted followers, Gandhi could perform a miracle.

What we know impressed the British was the performance of the Indian Army in both World Wars, which was not only outstanding but also crucial to British victory. This has not been given its due recognition in nationalist histories. Not so much nonviolence, but efficient military performance might have induced the British to acknowledge the debt the Empire owed to India. But that may not suit the Congress view of Indian history. The Montagu-Chelmsford Reforms were the first instalment, followed by the Simon Commission, the Round Table Conference, and the 1935 Act—a continuous chain of activity from Westminster concerning the governance of India. Then, another war intervened, and after that came Indian Independence.

What we have, instead, even to this day, is the story that it was the Congress Party which single-handedly delivered freedom under the leadership of Gandhi and Nehru. The Congress rejected the two-nation theory, but Jinnah was supported by the British in their quest to divide and rule.

There are problems with this stance. Thus in May 1947, Nehru and Patel agreed with Mountbatten that Partition was the only way out. Maulana Azad has told us in his book *India Wins Freedom* of Nehru's statement on 10 July 1946, which destroyed the decision agreed upon by all sides, along with the Cabinet Mission. When the book was published in 1959, it led to an immense debate, but no one has argued that Azad misquoted Nehru. Once that was said (somewhat unthinkingly), the old agreement unravelled, and Jinnah's Day of Action unleashed a storm.

Even so, let us persist and ask: why was Mountbatten in such a hurry? Indeed, why did Attlee set up the deadline of April 1948? What was the rush? Could they not have waited for emotions to calm down, and then reopen the negotiations? After all, impossible though it may sound now, 1958 would have marked the centenary of British rule over India. Wavell wanted to hang on.

Let us start with British impatience. What is not appreciated in the Indian debate is that Britain had just fought an exhausting, expensive war—the Second World War—within 30 years. It was bankrupt in terms of its gold reserves, and had lost its prime position. Having dominated the globe since the Battle of Waterloo, and established *pax Britannica* in 1815, it was now (at most) second to its former colony—the US. The Second World War, following the Great Depression, made it clear that while the ordinary people were willing to fight for king and country, they expected their condition to improve. The old aristocratic class, which had barely survived ignominy during the First World War, had to go, and reform was needed urgently to sustain democratic demands.

Democracy, especially universal franchise, had been galloping ahead during the twentieth century. When Edmund Burke wrote a diatribe against the French Revolution and defended British liberty, only two per cent of adult males had the franchise. During the First World War, all male adults and all women above 30 got the franchise. Then by 1928, all women got the franchise on the same basis as the men. Thus began the phase of democracy with universal franchise in Britain. It was this which came to fruition with the victory of the Labour Party and the demand for a welfare state. To the working people, the Empire did not mean as much as it did to the feudal classes.

Hence, the triumph of the Labour Party which split on the eve of the Second Round Table Conference after MacDonald's defection to form the National Government on the king's invitation. Churchill might have been the war hero, but he was discarded for tackling peacetime challenges. The Labour Party came to power with a genuine commitment to quitting India. Not so much for the love of Gandhi or Nehru, but because domestic problems were urgent. Housing and health, and building a welfare state, were top priority. Labour wanted to be out of India as soon as it could. India might have released 'a drain' in the preceding centuries, but not so much in the twentieth century, especially during the Depression, for Britain to hang on. Hence, the beginning of decolonization, with India first in the queue.

With hindsight, you could argue that as Jinnah was terminally sick, as the British secret service would have known, a few more years of hanging on might have saved an undivided India to become independent. But again, there was no certainty of the time of Jinnah's departure. The British people had voted Churchill out, and Attlee in, to get the work done. This was the urgency from the British end. There was little desire to postpone their departure. If there had to be some rethinking and a delay, the demand had to come from India. There the leaders—the younger generation which had come on the scene after the First World War—were in a hurry.

Back to a Divided British India

Getting back to our story, one has to probe further. British India witnessed the first and most sophisticated independence movement of any colony in the British Empire. From the establishment of the Indian National Congress in 1885, there came clever, knowledgeable Indians fighting for self-government, at first politely and then aggressively. When they won, it opened the floodgates for decolonization around the globe. But at home, it sparked a debate about why the Partition had to take place, and why British India broke up into India and Pakistan. This debate has not lost its salience yet.

Did they get it wrong? Was there one nation-state contained in British India or two? Were there just two nations or two nation-states? For Jinnah, the oldest and the richest Muslim community was in the Doab region of North India, the home of the Nawab of Awadh—the last Muslim kingdom taken over by the East India Company in the 1850s. However, while being a populous area, it was also a Muslim-minority area. It was this region which the Congress valued as the meeting ground of a syncretic Indian culture of Hindus and Muslims, and the Hindu nationalists celebrate as Hindu homeland nowadays!

The problem was, of course, that India was not just a country. It was, as Jinnah himself had said to Gandhi, a subcontinent.

Hindus and Muslims were spread all over India. But as any reading of its history would have shown, the bulk of Muslims were in the north, more particularly the frontier regions and those ruled by the Delhi Sultanate (roughly from 1100 to 1525), and then spreading to Central India (under the Mughals from 1526 to 1707); South India did not have much Muslim presence (except in the area now known as Kerala). Western India—Gujarat and Maharashtra—also had a sparse Muslim population. It was the language which distinguished one region from another.

If you were to add language to religion in defining a nation, you get a much more multinational collection across India as is the case in Europe, which has many nations with distinct languages but a population size smaller than that of India. In a way, this was proved by the 1971 divorce of East Pakistan from West Pakistan, and the former's rebirth as Bangladesh—giving clear prominence to language. Recalling what happened under Curzon at that time, the Partition of Bengal was resented by the Hindus of West Bengal, but welcomed by East Bengali Muslims. In a way, our story has been a subordinate story of the Bengal Partition (1905), its rejoining (1911), the repartition (1947), independence as a Bengali Muslim nation and a province of secular India in 1971.

Another nationality which has fizzled with discontent, but not reached a Bangladesh-like situation, is the Sikh people. They were a minority in Old India, but they could also claim to be a nation. Indeed, during the 1970s there was a movement for establishing a Sikh nation—Khalistan, as it is called—which created a climate of extralegal violence. Indira Gandhi, the prime minister in those years, was accused of encouraging the movement to damage rival parties in Punjab. If so, she paid a heavy price for this when she was shot at by one of her Sikh bodyguards. A horrendous massacre of Sikhs followed her death in New Delhi in December 1984. Hindus slaughtered Sikhs while the ruling Congress government made sure that the police stayed in their quarters, and did not intervene. Despite this horrible event, while Punjab was subjected to a heavy anti-terrorism regime, it did not get to a Bangladesh-like situation. There is a feeble Khalistan movement for a Sikh nation, more powerful among the Sikh diaspora than at home.

So, whatever was lost in 1947, the puzzle of Indian nationhood remained, perhaps not openly or officially, but as a debatable point. Jinnah and Gandhi tried to square the circle, but, despite themselves, failed.

The question of how many nations there were in (pre-1947) India remains unanswered. There was a tendency in the 1858–1947 period to assert that the answer was just one. But did it mean India had only one religion? That was obviously false. A change has come over more recently, though for 50 years after Independence, the Indian leadership defined secularism as the official doctrine, and India was cast as a nation with at least two religions, Hinduism and Islam, if not three, adding Sikhism, and then four with Buddhism due to Dr Ambedkar's public conversion, along with the untouchable community in the mid-1950s.

Now the pendulum has swung back, and a single religion—a Hindu nation—is being asserted. It is also argued that this one nation had preceded the arrival of the British, not to say the Muslim arrival since the advent of Islam. The farther back you go, the nation gets more uniformly defined as Hindu. This is, even so, a rewriting of history as for almost 1,500 years—from the middle of the fifth century BCE to the end of the first millennium of the Common Era—Buddhism, along with other Ajivika sects which were hostile to Hinduism, coexisted with Hinduism. This history has been forgotten or redefined by saying that Buddhism was a branch of Hinduism.

The nature of Indian nationhood is not a problem which will ever have a settled solution. As we noticed, over the course of Jinnah's life his opinions changed from believing in a single India to at least a two-nation theory. He won, though in a manner that was not satisfying to him or to the point he was making. Now of course there are three nation-states in the place of Old British India. Gandhi, on the other hand, stuck to his ecumenical theory of many religions in India. He lost his life for that idea.

BIBLIOGRAPHY

Ahmad, Ishtiaq, *Jinnah: His Successes, Failures and Role in History,* Penguin Viking, Gurgaon, India, 2020.

Akbar, M.J., *Gandhi's Hinduism: The Struggle Against Jinnah's Islam,* Bloomsbury, London, 2020.

Bolitho, Hector, *Jinnah: Creator of Pakistan,* John Murray, London, 1954.

Canadine, David, *Class in Britain,* Penguin, Middlesex, London, 1998.

Desai, Kishwar, *Jallianwala Bagh, 1919: The Real Story,* Harper Collins, Delhi, 2019.

Desai, Meghnad, *Development and Nationhood: Essays in the Political Economy of South Asia,* Oxford, New Delhi, 2005.

Desai, Meghnad, *Rethinking Islamism: The Ideology of the New Terror,* I.B. Tauris, London, 2007. Gandhi, Gopal, *The Oxford Gandhi: Essential Writings,* Oxford University Press, New Delhi, 2008.

Desai, Meghnad, *The Rediscovery of India,* Penguin Random House, Gurgaon, India, 2009.

Desai, Meghnad, *Who Wrote the Bhagavad Gita: A Secular Enquiry into a Sacred Text,* HarperCollins, Delhi, 2014.

Gandhi, M.K., *An Autobiography: or The Story of My Experiments with Truth,* Mahadev Desai (trans.), Navjivan, Ahmedabad, 1927/2004.

Godse, Gopal, and Nathuram Godse, *Why I Assassinated Gandhi,* Farsight Publishers and Distributors, Delhi, 2020.

Goradia, Prafull, *Jinnah Helped the Hindus and Other Explorations,* Vitasta, New Delhi, 2020.

Guha, Ramachandra, *Gandhi Before India,* Penguin Random House, Gurgaon, 2013.

Guha, Ramachandra, *Gandhi: The Years that Changed the World: 1914-1918,* Penguin Random House, Gurgaon, 2018.

His Majesty's Stationery Office, *Indian Round Table Conference (SECOND SESSION) 7th September, 1931—1st December, 1931, PROCEEDINGS,* January 1932, https://tinyurl.com/59mxuba6. Accessed on 10 April 2024.

Hunt, James D., *Gandhi in London,* Promilla Books, New Delhi, 2012.

Jalal, Ayesha, *The Sole Spokesman: Jinnah, the Muslim League and the Demand for Pakistan,* Cambridge University Press, New Delhi, 1985.

Marquand, David, *Ramsay MacDonald: A Political Biography,* MacMillan, 1977.

Mehta, Ved, *Mahatma Gandhi and His Apostles,* Penguin, London, 1977.

Mosley, Leonard, *Curzon: The End of an Epoch,* Readers Union, Longman Green & co., London, 1961.

Pakenham, Thomas, *The Boer War,* Weidenfeld and Nicholson, London, 1979.

Rowland, Peter, *Lloyd George: A Biography,* Macmillan, New York, 1975.

Sayyid, Matlubul Hasan, *Jinnah: A Political Study*, Shaikh Muhammad, Lahore, 1945.

Tidrick, Kathryn, *Gandhi: A Political and Spiritual Life*, I.B. Tauris, London, 2006.

Wolpert, Stanley, *Jinnah of Pakistan*, Oxford University Press, New York, 1984.

Yagnik, A., and S. Sheth, *The Shaping of Modern Gujarat: Plurality, Hindutva and Beyond*, Penguin, Delhi, 2005.

ACKNOWLEDGEMENTS

I have benefitted, as always in my efforts at writing books which require research, from the libraries which are vital to such tasks. In this case, I have enjoyed the use of the Nehru Memorial Library (as it was called when I used it) at Teen Murti in New Delhi, and my usual support from the House of Lords Library which prepared for me the documents on the Round Table Conference.

www.ingramcontent.com/pod-product-compliance
Lightning Source LLC
Chambersburg PA
CBHW020346100426
42812CB00035B/3378/J